True Type Tales

True Type Tales

Real Stories About the Power of Personality Type in Everyday Life

Patrick L Kerwin

ISBN 978-0-615-60927-0

FIRST EDITION
First printed 2013

Table of Contents

Introduction

Every day we encounter, observe, or interact with a variety of personalities – some that seem similar to us, some that seem quite different, and some that seem like they're from a different planet altogether! And you've undoubtedly experienced times when your natural style has worked well interacting with some people, and completely backfired when interacting with others. Well there's something that can transform how successfully you interact with *all* the people in your life – family, friends, coworkers, clients, and even complete strangers: A knowledge of the system of *personality type*.

I've used this system of personality type professionally and personally for over 20 years. In that time I've helped thousands of people understand their own personality type, the personality types of others, and how to use that knowledge to improve their personal relationships, their work relationships, and their everyday lives. In the course of using personality type in leadership development programs, team-building workshops, and coaching sessions, I've had the privilege of working with some amazing organizations including Google, Microsoft, Heinz, Amgen, Suncor Energy, the UC San Francisco Center for the Health Professions, Monarch HealthCare, the San Diego County District Attorney's Office, the U.S. Navy, the University of Notre Dame, and Purdue University. And I've also had the privilege of working with some amazing individuals from a wide variety of occupations, including rocket scientists (literally!), university presidents, bus drivers, corporate CEOs, community college counselors, physicians, accountants, district attorneys, you name it. And what they all discovered through our work with personality type was this: Making *incremental* changes in your behaviors can create *monumental* changes in your interactions at work and at home.

I use my knowledge of personality type every single day as I manage my business and lead my personal life. In fact, "type" is so engrained in how I view the world, people, and interactions, not a day goes by that I don't see type in action. And believe it or not, I don't go looking for it! But what happens is that type comes *at* me from the things people do and say. Like the boy in the movie "The Sixth Sense" who said, "I see dead people," well, "I see *type people*."

Because I have worked with type for over 20 years, I have a *lot* of examples of type in action. I use those examples to illustrate type when I conduct my workshops and training programs, and people usually enjoy them. For years, workshop participants would say to me, "You should write a book with all your stories." I didn't take that too seriously at first, but then I started hearing people say things like, "That example you gave really helped me understand my [spouse, partner, parent, child, boss, co-worker, friend] so much better," or "When you gave that one example, it made it so clear to me why I'm having problems with this one person at work." So I started jotting down my examples, and before I knew it, I realized I had more than enough stories to form an entire book.

And now I understand why those examples are so powerful. First, they're not hypothetical or fabricated in order to fit a theory of how personalities are "supposed" to work. They are *real* stories of personality type happening in everyday situations. Second, because these stories are real and deal with topics like relationships, work, family, and friendships, they are stories that everyone can relate to. And third, stories about people's personalities and how they use them aren't only insightful and useful, they're also often downright amusing!

So let's get started…

Chapter 1
The Language of Personality Type

Over the years there have been many theories and models developed to explain and describe personalities and how they operate. The stories in this book are presented through the lens of one of the most enduring theories of personality – the theory of psychological types – created by C.G. Jung in 1921, and popularized by the Myers-Briggs Type Indicator® (MBTI®) personality assessment.

Jung's theory explains the normal differences that exist among people, and provides language for understanding those differences. The premise of the theory is that each of us, at our core, is 'hard-wired' to have preferences for doing things in certain ways, sort of like being left-handed or right-handed.

Here's a great example. Grab a pen or pencil, and on the line below, sign your signature as you normally would:

____

What words would you use to describe the act of signing your signature?

I know, it seems like an odd question! You may be thinking, "I don't know how to describe it. It's just what I do." Or maybe you thought of a few words like "automatic," "easy," or "comfortable."

OK, now sign your name below with your *other* hand:

____

What words would you use to describe the act of signing your signature with that hand?

I'll bet you came up with a lot more words! You might have thought of words like "difficult," "uncomfortable," "awkward," "childlike," "slow," or "it took a lot of concentration." And you may have even laughed, or thought, "I can't even do this!"

This example illustrates what Jung's theory of personality types is all about. From years of observing peoples' behaviors, Jung found that each of us has a preference for certain parts of our personality, much like you have a natural preference for writing with one hand over the other. In addition, Jung also found that each of us have parts of our personality that are *not* our preference, much like using your other hand to write.

When you use those parts of your personality that are your natural preferences, it's like writing with your preferred hand – easy, automatic, and comfortable. In fact, it can be so natural, you might not even realize you're doing it or know how to describe it – or, you might think, "It's so natural for me, surely *everyone* must do it this way too!"

Conversely, when you use those parts of your personality that are *not* your preference, it's like writing with your non-preferred hand – uncomfortable, awkward, childlike, slow, and it takes a lot of concentration. And because it's so unnatural, you often *really* notice when you're using those non-preferred parts of your personality.

In addition, guess what happens when *others* have natural preferences that are the opposite of yours? You also tend to *really* notice it, and often have a *lot* of words to describe the way they're doing things – such as "difficult," "awkward," and "childlike!"

The language of personality type preferences used in this book addresses four different aspects of your personality, each with two opposite ways of doing things, much like being right-handed or left-handed. Those four aspects are:

- What energizes you
- What kind of information you like and trust
- How you make decisions
- How you approach life

For each aspect, you'll likely have a preference for one over its opposite. Knowing your preferences can help explain what you most naturally "reach for first" in your personality – which in turn can help explain why you do things in certain ways, and how others might do them differently.

As you think about your own personality, there are a couple of important things to remember about personality preferences. First, just like having a preference for one hand doesn't mean you can't or don't use your opposite hand, having a preference for doing things one way doesn't mean you can't or don't use the opposite preference. Each of us uses all parts of our personality;

we just tend to have a preference for certain parts over their opposites. Second, just like having a preference for one hand isn't any better or worse than having a preference for the other hand, there aren't any "better" or "worse" personality preferences. Each preference has its own assets, and presents its own challenges as well.

As you go through this book, you'll read descriptions of the two opposites associated with each aspect of personality, and then read real stories about those preferences as they appear in real life. After you finish each chapter, you'll decide which preference sounds more naturally like you.

As you read and contemplate your own personality preferences, it's important to think about your most natural preferences. Try to filter out things like:

- Who other people think you are
- How you "have to be" in order to be successful at work

or at home

- What you've been trained to be or rewarded to be
- Who you're trying to become
- Who you think you "should be"
- Who you wish you were

We're trying to drill down beyond those factors to figure out your most natural preferences – the ones that are truly "you."

At the end of the book, you'll learn tips and strategies for making the best use of your four preferences, and for using personality type to enrich and improve your life, both personally and professionally.

Chapter 2
What Energizes You

The first aspect of personality type explains your natural source of energy: Extraversion or Introversion. In personality type language, letters are used as shorthand for identifying the whole words. In this case, Extraversion is referred to as "E," and Introversion is referred to as "I."

Of all the words used to describe personality types, "extravert" and "introvert" are the ones we encounter most often in everyday language. You hear it all the time:

"She's such an extravert."

"He's so introverted."

Often people think of extraverts as people who are outgoing, gregarious, or loud, and of introverts as people who are shy, introspective, or quiet. And while some of those everyday descriptions of extraverts and introverts are similar to the personality type descriptions of those two words, there are some distinct differences as well.

Let's take a look at the personality type descriptions for E and I, which address *what energizes you.*

People with a preference for E:

- Are energized by the outer world of things, people, or activities that take place around them
- Tend to direct more of their energy outward
- Figure things out by talking them out
- Can be social and talkative with people they've just met as well as people they know well – and when talking about almost any topic

People with a preference for I:

- Are energized by the inner world of ideas, thoughts, and reflections that take place inside them
- Tend to direct more of their energy inward
- Figure things out by thinking them through
- Can be social and talkative with people they know well, or when they have great interest in the topic or person

As you see, in type language, not all E's are loud, and not all I's are shy. The real difference between E's and I's is what *energizes* them.

You'll probably see parts of yourself in both the E and I descriptions, since we all use both the Extraverted and Introverted parts of ourselves. But the question you'll be trying to answer is not which one you *do*, but which one is your *natural preference.*

Before you decide, read the following E – I stories. As you read them, you'll likely find yourself identifying with one preference more than the other. Then at the end of this chapter, you'll have an opportunity to select the preference that sounds most like you.

Down Time

While each of us has a preference for getting energized primarily by the outer world of Extraversion or by the inner world of Introversion, we also know that everyone does *both*. So those of you who have a preference for E are Introverting right now by reading this book, and those of you who have a preference for I will be Extraverting when you discuss with your family and friends how fascinating this book is!

In fact, regardless of your preference for E or I, spending time in both your Extraverted *and* Introverted worlds is important to maintain balance in your personality. For example, people who spend all of their time Extraverting without spending some time Introverting can become burned out and exhausted. And people who spend all of their time Introverting without spending some time Extraverting can become overly-isolated and detached.

One thing that both E's and I's need is down time. But the main differentiating factor between E's and I's is *how much* down time they need after a day filled with a great deal of Extraverting, such as interacting with many people during a day, or being in meetings with others for most of the day. After a day of such Extraverting, even E's will say they need some Introverted down time, but I's often describe needing much more.

In one four-day MBTI training program I conducted in San Francisco, there was a man who reported E on his MBTI personality assessment, and who agreed with that preference for the first three days of the program. When we did E-I activities, he fit in quite naturally with the other E's, and, well, let's just say, if you had met him those first three days, there would have been little mystery about his preference for E!

On the fourth day, however, he walked into the room and announced to the group that he realized overnight that he really had a preference for I. His proclamation caught all of us by great surprise since he had given off very few Introverted behavioral cues during the week. However, I am a firm believer that every person has the right to decide on his or her own personality preferences, regardless of how well other people might think those preferences fit. But when someone's behavior doesn't match his or her preference, I'm also very curious about what might be causing the apparent disconnect.

So I asked him the obvious question: "What prompted the switch from E to I?"

And he replied, "I realized that after a big day at work, when I've been really busy or I've been talking to a bunch of people, I need down time."

I explained to him that both E's and I's need down time after a day of Extraverting. "But," I said, "Here's the big question: How *much* down time do you need?"

And he said, "After a really big day at work, I need a good half an hour. Then I'm ready to go!"

We all burst into laughter, but the Introverts in the room laughed louder. Because if you have a preference for I, half an hour is only *beginning* to scratch the surface of down time!

Gold Coins

Because the E and I preferences are about energy, it's helpful to think about how we get it, and how we spend it – just like money. In fact, you can think about energy like gold coins, with each of us having a bag in which we carry our coins – and each bag gets filled up and depleted in different ways!

Here's how it works for people who have a preference for E:

When E's first wake up in the morning, they've just finished an evening of little interaction with their outer world. Because they've just been sleeping, E's haven't been gathering much energy from their outer world, and hence, they haven't been gathering many gold coins either. In other words: When E's first wake up, their bag of gold coins is empty!

But then let's say an E walks outside and sees a neighbor.

"Hey, how's it going, neighbor?" the E says.

"Fine," the neighbor replies. And with that reply, the E gets some energy, and hence a few gold coins drop into the E's bag.

"Got any plans for the weekend?" the E asks.

"Yes, we're going away to the lake for a couple of days," the neighbor replies. And a few more gold coins drop into the E's bag.

And with each interaction the E has during the day, a few more gold coins go into the bag. With enough of those interactions, the E's bag is full, and the E is rich with energy.

Now here's how it works for people who have a preference for I:

When I's first wake up in the morning, they've just finished an evening away from the distractions of their outer environment. Because they've been sleeping, I's have been gathering energy from their inner world, and hence, have been gathering gold coins at the same time. In other words: When I's first wake up in the morning, their bag of gold coins is full!

Now let's play out that same exchange between neighbors from above, but from an I's perspective.

"Hey, how's it going neighbor?" the neighbor asks.

"Fine," the I replies. And with that reply, the I uses up some energy, and pays out a few gold coins.

"Got any plans for the weekend?" the neighbor asks.

"Yes, we're going away to the lake for a couple of days," the I replies, shelling out a few more gold coins.

And with each Extraverted interaction the I has during the day, a few more gold coins get spent out of the bag. And if an I has enough of those Extraverted interactions, at the end of the day the I's bag is empty, and the I is out of energy.

By the way, it works in the opposite direction as well. When E's spend a great deal of time in Introverted environments, they pay out as well!

What's your bag like?

Depth vs. Breadth

My partner Scott has a preference for Introversion, and I have a preference for Extraversion. This combination provides no shortage of type stories! One of those happened last year when we both had medical appointments on the same day. Scott had an appointment to see a periodontist for a consultation, and I had an appointment to see a physician's assistant for a minor medical procedure.

At the end of the day, we compared notes on our medical visits. Because my brain tends to process interactions in terms of personality type, I naturally asked Scott, "So do you think your periodontist would have guessed your preference to be E or I?" (Yes, these are the kinds of questions I ask!)

Scott, by virtue of our relationship, has become something of an MBTI aficionado in his own right, so he didn't miss a beat. He replied, "Even though I'm an Introvert, I think she would have guessed that I was an Extravert."

"Really!" I said, intrigued. "Why's that?"

"During the consultation," he said, "she described the procedure I was going to have done. It was a laser procedure, and we started discussing the equipment she would be using. It turns out that my company manufactures a component used in that equipment, so I talked a lot about our manufacturing process, and then we talked about the different lasers she uses in her practice and the different components that are used in each machine. I talked a lot, so I think she would have guessed me to be an Extravert."

"Wow, it sounds like you really did talk a lot," I said. "Well just for contrast, here's what an Extravert sounds like in a medical appointment." And I began to tell him about my visit with the physician's assistant.

"I walked into the procedure room, the Physician's Assistant introduced herself, explained the procedure, and asked if I had any questions. I said no, so she got started. Then I asked her how long she's been a PA. I learned she's been a PA for 10 years, and that she went to the University of Arizona. That prompted me to ask her if she grew up there, but it turns out she actually grew up in Colorado. I talked about our friend who lives in Denver, and how beautiful it is there. Then I asked her how long she's been in San Diego. She mentioned she and her fiancé moved here 8 years ago and that they love it. I asked her when they're getting married, and found out they're getting married in one year in Hawaii, on the Big Island. I told her you and I are going there to celebrate my birthday next month! So we talked about the Big Island and what resort they'll be staying at, and it turns out it's right up the road from ours! And then the procedure was done."

"Wow," he said. "You talked about a *lot.*"

I replied, "I did?"

This story is a great example that both E's *and* I's can be extremely talkative – just in different ways! E's tend to be talkative with people they know well and also with people they don't know well, and about topics they know well and also topics they don't know well! I's tend to be talkative with people they know well or are interested in, or about topics they know well or are interested in. It's when I's don't know the person well (or aren't interested), or don't know the topic well (or aren't interested) that they tend to be quiet. As a result, E's often have conversations of great breadth, while I's tend to have conversations of great depth.

So "talking" alone isn't the barometer of someone's preference for Extraversion or Introversion. It's *what* they're talking about, and *with whom*!

Extraverting My Way Through Customs

I do quite a bit of work in Canada. Whenever you visit a foreign country for work, you naturally expect a lot of questions from the local customs officers about what kind of work you'll be doing there and why you're doing it. Because the idea of personality type workshops can be hard to explain quickly, I always find those kinds of questions very hard to answer. And yet as someone who has a preference for Extraversion, I am naturally drawn like the moth to the flame to verbally attempt to explain what I do, and to throw in a bonus response of elaborating on my reasons for entering their country.

The consistent problem has been that if I say I work with personality types, people either think I am a psychiatrist or immediately get nervous that I am sizing up their personality (which *most* of the time, I really am not). I can't tell you the number of times I have heard, "Oh yeah, then what type of personality am I?" (Which is just *begging* for a sarcastic response, and which – given the situation – I restrain myself from providing!) So despite trying my best to give a concise description of what I do, I somehow run aground and end up giving a convoluted explanation – which invariably results in being sent to secondary customs for more questioning. As you might imagine, this problem began creating a great deal of anxiety for me with each work trip to Canada I made.

Meanwhile, the company that brings me to Canada to conduct the MBTI Certification Program has – since my first trip for them 10 years ago – provided me with a beautifully and thoroughly written letter addressed to the Canadian customs agency. In that letter are specifics and details about the kind of work I do, why I'll be doing it there, where I'll be staying, and their contact information should there be any questions or concerns. And for years I have taken the letter with me on each trip, and simply kept it tucked away in case I needed it.

And finally it dawned on me: the process of customs usually involves the quiet and careful review of documentation and paperwork. And as a result, it's natural that most people who are drawn to that kind of work would likely have a preference for Introversion. And yet there I was, trying to *Extravert* my way through a process that is actually quite *Introverted!*

So last year on a work trip to Canada, I decided to take a different approach. As I approached the front of the customs line, I repeated this mantra to myself: "Keep it Introverted." When the customs officer motioned me over, I walked up and presented my entry document and passport.

"You're here for work?" she asked.

"Yes, and here's a letter," I said, doing my best to Introvert and use few words (as mentioned earlier, *not* my virtue). I presented the letter from the Canadian company, and she began to read it carefully. As she read it, I found myself wanting to explain the letter and to elaborate on my situation. Surely she needed more explanation! But I remembered my mantra, and bit my tongue.

"Thank you," she said, as she stamped my passport, returned my documents, and waved up the next person in line.

Thinking it might have been a fluke, when I returned to Canada for work a few months later, I decided to try my Introverted system again. It worked like a charm.

Doors and Type

There's an activity that is often used in workshops to illustrate the differences between Extraversion and Introversion at work. The people who have a preference for E assemble together in one group and the people who have a preference for I assemble in another, and each group comes up with their responses to the question, "What do you like in a work environment?"

The responses you typically hear from the E group include, "Working with people," "Being able to float around the office," and "Lots of activity." The responses you typically hear from the I group include, "Working on my own," "Having few interruptions," and "Being able to focus."

In one workshop, however, both groups came up with one identical response: "Having a door to close." That is something you expect to hear from the I group, but not from the E group! But if you believe in type, which I do, unexpected responses usually have an explanation that doesn't negate personality type theory, but actually supports it.

So I asked the I group, "Why do you like having a door to close?" They responded, "To keep other people *out.* If people keep coming in, we'll never get any work done!"

Then I said to the E group, "Your response was a little surprising to me. Why do *you* like having a door to close?" And they responded, "To keep ourselves *in.* If we don't close our doors, we'll always be out and about and we'll never get any work done!"

And *that* makes perfect sense.

Extraversion & Nap Time

People often ask how soon you can tell the type preferences of children. Some people say you can tell quite early, others say it takes time. In my case, you could tell when I was in kindergarten.

When I went to kindergarten, part of the day was spent in nap time. This was the time when you would take out a mat, lie on the floor, try to sleep, and give your exhausted teacher a break. Given my preference for Extraversion, this was *not* my favorite part of school.

One day during nap time, I thought a far more engaging activity would be to talk to the boy next to me about my favorite television show. And that was when I got kicked out of kindergarten class for talking.

I was sent out into the hallway (with the poor kid I was talking to), and remember being confused on why I was being punished. It wasn't until years later, when I learned about type, that I figured out what had happened. I had been Extraverting, when I was supposed to be *Introverting!*

Fortunately I was able to put this lesson to use many years later when Kaile, my friend Patti's daughter, came home from elementary school one day in tears. "What happened?" we asked.

"I'm a blabbermouth!" she cried.

"Who told you that?" we asked.

"The kids in my class. I got in trouble for talking during class, so all the kids called me a blabbermouth," she said.

Now I have known Kaile since she was one, and I always suspected she had a preference for Extraversion (she has since confirmed that by taking the MBTI instrument in college). So I told Kaile my story about getting kicked out of kindergarten, and how there are some kids that like to talk to learn. I assured her there was nothing wrong with that – unless the talking happens when you're supposed to be quiet. I told her that I, too, had to learn when it was okay to talk, and when it wasn't.

"So you're not a blabbermouth, Kaile," I said, "You're an Extravert!" It actually seemed to help, and we still laugh about that story today. So there ended up being some benefit to my getting kicked out of kindergarten after all!

Oh, and to the boy who got kicked out with me: Sorry about that.

<u>Extraversion & School – Again</u>

The community I grew up in experienced tremendous growth as I was entering elementary school. By the time I started 4th grade, there weren't enough classrooms to accommodate the number of students in attendance. Since this surge of students was temporary, it didn't warrant building a permanent addition to the school, so a set of several temporary classrooms was erected adjacent to the school. These "pods," as they were called, held approximately 120 students each. Students were then rotated between traditional classrooms and the pods, ensuring that every student would spend part of the day in a traditional classroom, and part of the day in a pod.

In one of the pods, the desks were arranged to form three large U-shapes, one within the other. The outer one had about 50 desks, the next one in had about 40, and the next one in had about 30. In the center of the "U" were four tables which formed a small square, in which stood the four teachers who taught the class. Because of the size of the room, the teachers used a microphone to teach the class (yes, it was the '70s!). This was the pod that provided me with yet my second encounter with Extraversion in the classroom.

I have no recollection of the subject being taught that day, but I do remember that it was Cookie Day. That meant at the end of class, all the students were dismissed to the cafeteria where we would have the treat of eating free cookies. And I also remember – due to the events of that day – the name of the kid who sat next to me. His name was Mark K.

So there we were, all 120 of us, listening to one of the teachers deliver her lesson. And there I was again, a kid with a preference for Extraversion, finding it much more interesting to chat with Mark K. than to listen to the lesson being taught.

I remember leaning back in my chair, talking to Mark K., when suddenly I heard my name. It came from the teacher's voice over the microphone, but it sounded just like the teacher's voice in those Charlie Brown specials: "Bwah bwah bwah bwah Patrick Kerwin?" And because I had been talking, I had absolutely *no* idea what she had asked.

Panicked, I turned to Mark K.

"What's the answer?" I asked.

He quickly told me what to say, and I blurted out my answer to all 120 students and four teachers.

"FIVE!" I shouted, proudly.

At which point the entire class of 120 students broke into laughter.

The four teachers did not.

The teacher responded, "I'll see you after class."

I met with her after class, at which time I learned the question she had asked. And that question had been: "How many legs does a chair have, Patrick Kerwin?"

Needless to say, I was *not* allowed to attend Cookie Day.

And once again, Extraversion had bitten me in the behind at school.

And to Mark K., wherever you are: I've forgiven you. Sort of.

People & Introversion

In one MBTI workshop I conducted, the topic came up about the connection between having a preference for E or I and liking people. The conversation focused on the question, "Are E's the only people who like people, or do I's like people too?"

There was a great deal of discussion, and of course the answer was that both E's and I's like people, they just interact with them in different ways.

After the discussion, one woman with a preference for Introversion came up to me to share a comment with me privately (in true Introversion style).

"I just wanted you to know, I like people," she said.

"OK," I said, wondering where this was going.

She continued, "I like reading about them and watching them in movies." And she smiled and walked away.

That is classic Introverted humor: subtle, with few words – and hilarious!

Culture and E & I

In an MBTI training program I conducted in New York, the question came up about how culture affects one's preference for E or I. We discussed that although your preference for E or I is innate, culture can influence how you *express* that preference. I used the example of the U.K., where the cultural norm is to be reserved and Introverted. So when someone who has a preference for E in the U.K. starts Extraverting, that Extraversion preference passes through a culture filter that says, "That's not how we do things here." As a result, that person may display more Introverted behaviors because of the cultural norm – while still fully having a preference for Extraversion.

Right after that conversation, a participant said he had a great example for the group. He explained to the group that although he might appear to be an I, he actually had a preference for E. He went on to explain that for the past 20 years he had lived in Finland, and in order to be a successful business person in Finland you had to act more Introverted, otherwise people there wouldn't take you seriously. It was a great example of how each of us uses both our preferred and non-preferred preferences, and how we might even use our less-preferred preferences regularly when they can help us succeed or fit in.

He then went on to explain more about the Finnish culture, and the difference between Extraverts and Introverts in Finland. Here's what he said:

"In Finland, Extraverts are the people who look at *your* shoes when they talk to you. And Introverts are the people who look at *their* shoes when they talk to you!"

We all had a good laugh. But it also prompted all of us in the room to reflect on our own culture and family norms. Did our cultural or family norms encourage Extraversion or Introversion? And how did those norms match our own preference for E or I?

How about for you?

Debriefing Your Day

Because the Extraversion and Introversion preferences address communication, it's not long in any workshop before someone says, "That explains so much about my [husband, wife, partner]!"

To frame up this story, it's helpful to remember one of the key differences between E's and I's: They process differently at the end of a day's work. When E's get home after a day at work, they often like to immediately debrief their day with others, reviewing and discussing the events of their day. Conversely, I's, having just spent all of their energy at work, often prefer to have some quiet time to regroup when they get home.

In one MBTI workshop I conducted in San Francisco, the group discussion soon turned to significant others and communication differences. After much discussion between E's and I's and what they need when they come home from work, one woman with a preference for Extraversion said, "I just figured out an interaction I had with my Introverted husband last week!"

She went on to tell us that, as an E, it was typical for her to come home from work and begin regaling her husband with all the events of her day. One day, in the middle of her Extraverted debrief, her husband, who as you will recall has a preference for Introversion, said:

"Stop. Pretend I have two minutes to live. What do I need to know? Go!"

We all broke into laughter, including her. "And honestly, he's a great guy and we have a really solid relationship!" she said, and we all believed her.

But then we talked about what we could learn from that story. As an E, her need to Extravert was real, and immediate. But she also had several options for getting her immediate Extraverted needs met in ways *other than* talking with her husband – calling a friend, or talking to a family member, for example – and then talking with him a little bit later.

Her husband, as an I, could only get his Introverted needs met in one way: by going inside himself for some quiet time. He wasn't being rude or insensitive – he just didn't have any more energy to give at that moment. And he'd be happy to hear all about her day… once he regained some energy.

Simple as that.

<u>Arm Crossing</u>

When you learn about personality type, you begin to realize how often we mistakenly assign meaning to other people's behaviors. What we tend to do is assign meaning to our behaviors, and then when we see someone else doing the same behavior, we assign *our* meaning to *their* behavior! That's called "projection," and it goes something like this:

A. When I do XYZ behavior, this is what it means for me.
B. Someone else is doing XYZ behavior.
C. This is what XYZ behavior means for them.

And the problem can occur when we make that leap from "what it means for me" to "what it means for them!"

For example, think about this:

You're in a meeting, and you have your arms crossed and are staring at the ceiling. What does that mean?

If you have a preference for E, that arm-crossing behavior usually means that you're disengaged, uninterested, irritated, or completely checked out.

However, if you have a preference for I, that arm-crossing behavior usually means that you're thinking, contemplating, or reflecting.

Alternatively, you could have a preference for E *or* I, and just be cold!

So here's how the type-related projection occurs:

If a person with a preference for E had been leading that meeting, and he or she saw the "Arm Crosser," that behavior would likely have been processed like this:

A. When I have my arms crossed, it means I'm disengaged or irritated.

B. Shannon has her arms crossed.

C. That means Shannon is disengaged or irritated. That's a problem!

However, if a person with a preference for I had been leading that same meeting, and he or she saw the "Arm Crosser," that behavior would likely have been processed like this:

A. When I have my arms crossed, it means I'm thinking or reflecting.

B. Shannon has her arms crossed.

C. That means Shannon is thinking or reflecting. That's good!

The true meaning of Shannon's behavior really depends on whether she has a preference for E or I – so the meeting leaders could have been right *or* wrong in their interpretation of Shannon's behavior.

If Shannon has a preference for E, then she could have indeed been disengaged or irritated. In that case, the E leader's conclusion would have been accurate, and the I leader's conclusion would have been an *inaccurate* introverted projection.

But if Shannon has a preference for I, then she may have indeed been fully engaged, and was thinking or reflecting. In that case, the I leader's conclusion would have been accurate, and the E leader's conclusion would have been an *inaccurate* extraverted projection.

So the moral of the story is: Be careful of your own projections when interpreting behaviors. Our projections are usually only accurate if the person we are projecting them onto has our same personality preference! If the person has the opposite preference, our interpretation could be all wrong.

And the second moral of the story is: Look for type projections in the models or theories you use. I'm convinced that whoever came up with the behavioral interpretation that "Having your arms crossed means you're defensive and closed" was someone who had a preference for Extraversion – because it's a classic Extraverted projection!

Interjecting

Speaking of projections, let's look at another one:

You're in a meeting and are interjecting your ideas, are quick to add on to, comment on, and elaborate on other peoples' statements, and are sometimes interrupting others. What does that mean?

If you have a preference for E, that kind of behavior usually means you are fully engaged, energized, and contributing!

However, if you have a preference for I, that kind of behavior usually means that you are very frustrated, somewhat annoyed, and feeling rather rude!

So here's how the projection occurs in this example:

If a person who has a preference for E is leading that meeting, and observes the "Interrupter," that behavior will likely be processed like this:

A. When I interrupt, it means I'm totally energized and engaged.
B. Shannon is interrupting.
C. That means Shannon is energized and engaged; that's great!

But if a person who has a preference for I is leading that same meeting and observes the "Interrupter," that behavior will likely be processed like this:

A. When I interrupt, it means I'm frustrated and being rude.
B. Shannon is interrupting.
C. That means Shannon is frustrated or rude; that's a problem!

And just like the previous story on projection, the accuracy of the projection will depend greatly on Shannon's preference for E or I.

By the way, when I's do interrupt in a conversation, it is often because they have listened to a lot of talking and have had a hard time "merging" into the conversation. Because of their frustration, they'll finally decide to interrupt the conversation, and will often do so quite forcefully, surprising the people around them. It's what I call the Introverted "That's it; I'm going in!" phenomenon!

Being an Introvert Sympathizer

In one MBTI workshop I conducted in Indiana, there was a wonderful, gentle woman with a preference for Introversion. As she learned more about her type throughout the workshop, she was finally able to make sense of something that had happened to her consistently when growing up.

In school, she said, she was often accused of being "stuck up" or appearing that she thought she was better than others. She never understood those comments, and found them very hurtful. It wasn't until she learned about her preference for I that she figured out that others were misinterpreting her quiet demeanor.

We went on to discuss that her quiet demeanor could have been misinterpreted as being judgmental of others – and that likely, that misinterpretation was happening from Extraverts. The reason for that? More projection! Sometimes, when E's are being quiet, it's because *they're* being judgmental. So when someone else is quiet? It's easy for an E to think, *"That person is being judgmental.*"

This woman's story, along with so many others I have heard from Introverts, is part of the reason why – even though I have a preference for Extraversion – I am an Introvert sympathizer. Here are some of the other reasons:

- E's are hardwired to do and say things immediately, while I's are hardwired to process internally before saying or doing things. Work and life are becoming increasingly immediate, which favors people with a preference for Extraversion.

- Because E's are wired to put themselves "out there," what you see is what you get. There's usually not a lot of mystery to what Extraverts are about, and as a result, rarely do E's describe being horribly misunderstood. And if you're an E and someone *does* misunderstand you, you'll usually engage with them to address the misunderstanding! Introverts, on the other hand, are naturally wired to keep "who they really are" tucked inside until they trust others or know them well. As a result, because people can't read them quickly, Introverts all over the world describe being misunderstood or misjudged.

- There is often an assumption that if you have something to say, you'll say it – which is a very E point of view! So if you have preference for I, and you tend to refine your ideas internally before speaking, people can misjudge your internal reflection time as not having anything to say. It's been said that if you don't know what an Extravert is thinking, you're not listening, and if you don't know what an Introvert is thinking, you haven't asked.

- I's often hear, "You never speak up," "You won't

> engage in conflict," or "You don't embrace change." And often, those comments are spoken from the lips of E's, who forget to add one word to the end of those sentences: "*immediately!*" It's not that I's don't have anything to say, don't want to engage in conflict, or don't embrace change – it's just that they need time to process internally *first.*

If you have a preference for Extraversion, don't slam this book shut yet! The responsibility for stretching outside of one's natural preferences doesn't belong to Extraverts alone. Introverts also have a responsibility to do the following:

- When you are processing internally, let people know that's what you're doing.

- Push an idea or thought into the external world before you have it fully formed or before it might be comfortable. Keeping the idea inside might mean your idea gets lost.

- Provide an immediate clue that you are engaged in the discussion, even if that clue is just saying that you're not ready to contribute immediately!

<u>Introversion and Silence</u>

I conducted an MBTI workshop for a team of career counselors in Tucson several years ago. While we were doing an E-I activity, the discussion came up regarding how long people could sit in silence with comfort. Many of the I's on the team described being comfortable spending long stretches of time in silence.

On that team were two people with a preference for I; one was the team manager, the other was a team member. During our conversation about silence, the I team member said this:

"I have a perfect example. Sometimes I go into my manager's office for a meeting, and we'll spend ten minutes sitting in complete silence, reflecting on an idea together." Her Introverted manager nodded.

The E's were shocked. "You mean you'll actually sit for that entire time and not say a single word to each other? Isn't that uncomfortable?"

The I's replied, "Yes, we'll sit there for the entire time. And no, it's not uncomfortable at all. Sometimes we'll sit for even longer."

At which point the E's began to twitch at the very thought!

Meditation

Shortly after I relocated to San Diego 14 years ago, I decided to go on a spiritual quest. As someone with a preference for Extraversion, I was seeking not only a place of spiritual connection, but also a place to meet people! Each week I selected a different faith or denomination, and visited the corresponding place of worship for its weekly service.

One Sunday I visited a place of worship in my neighborhood. Shortly into the service, we were asked to meditate. Now I've read and heard about all the benefits of meditation, but if you think about it, meditating is a rather Introverted activity. And while it might be beneficial, it's not a natural activity for someone like me who has a natural preference for Extraversion. And that's not to say that I don't do my own form of meditation – but it's more of an *Extraverted* form. So, for example, I might go to the beach, where there is some activity, and stare off into the ocean and quiet my mind – but with my eyes open. Some might say that doesn't count as meditation – but for an E, it does!

In any case, I decided to try the classical Introverted form of meditating at the service, and closed my eyes. "This isn't so bad," I thought. "Just relax, and let your mind be quiet. See, you're doing it!"

After what seemed like 20 minutes – but what I'm fairly certain was in actuality only 20 seconds – I couldn't stand it. "When are they going to call time?" I wondered. So I popped one eye open to take a look around the room. Certainly everyone was done meditating by now. As I peered around the room, however, I saw that everyone was still deep in meditation.

"OK, a little longer," I told myself, and closed my eyes. Once again, I relaxed my breathing, cleared my mind, and tried to create space for some spiritual exploration.

By now I thought I must have been there for close to a full hour, the service would be ending shortly, and I would have mastered meditation. But just to be sure, I popped my eye open once again to assess the situation. The first thing I did was glance at my watch, which revealed that I was in fact just a few minutes into the service. Peering around the room, I noticed that everyone I could see was still deep in meditation.

"How long can this go on?" I wondered to myself. The silence was deafening. I decided that I had taken sufficient baby steps into meditation, and finally just opened my eyes. It felt a little like cheating on a test, but I was actually quite interested in watching everyone meditate. They all seemed so calm and peaceful, which made me feel calm and peaceful too. After five more minutes of observation, I thought, "I think there's really something to the notion of an Extraverted from of meditation!"

Now some meditation purists might disagree. But you have to remember that for Extraverts, the concept of "complete comfort in silence" is like the axiom that says "one dog year is equivalent to seven human years." For E's, each minute of silence can seem like seven! So if you have a preference for E, go easy on yourself when you are trying to learn introverted activities. And if you have a preference for I, be patient with your Extraverted brethren as they try out Introverted activities.

Inquiring Minds

Because people with a preference for E tend to thrive on external input, they usually look and listen for cues of engagement when they're with others. Conversely, because people with a preference for I tend to thrive on internal processing, they usually listen and focus intently when they're with others. This can create one of the many sources of misunderstanding between E's and I's.

A classic example of this is when an E asks an I a question. As they ask the question, the E is looking for verbal or nonverbal cues that the I understands the question and is engaged in the conversation.

As they hear the question, however, the I is focusing on the question, and on processing the question internally. Because the focus is largely internal, the I often provides few verbal or nonverbal cue of understanding or engagement. Often, they look intently at the question-asker – which then becomes completely disorienting to the E. This then causes the E to think things like,

"Why are they staring at me? Why are they not saying anything? Oh, I know – they must not understand the question!"

And at that point, the E identifies the solution to the "problem": Use more words, and ask the question in different ways! So the E begins talking more, rephrasing the question. To which the I says to him- or herself, "I wish they'd stop talking for a minute! I got it the FIRST time; I'm just thinking!"

During a discussion of this phenomenon during an MBTI workshop, a group of I's came up with a wonderful analogy. Here's what they said to the E's:

"Remember the days when you had to use dial-up to access a website? Well when you E's ask us I's a question, it's like you typed in the web address and hit 'Enter.'

And remember how you used to see that little hour glass spinning around to show you that the website was loading? Well that hour glass is like us I's, processing your question.

And then when we don't come up with an immediate response – just like when websites didn't used to immediately load – what do you E's do? You start asking us the question in different ways to try and get an immediate answer – which is just like hitting, 'Enter, Enter, Enter, Enter!'

And then what happens? Just like what used to happen to websites back then: We freeze!"

So a lesson for the E's: Ask the question once. Do not hit "enter" again!

And lesson for the I's: Give a cue that you are processing. Make the hour glass bigger!

Enthusiasm

When people with a preference for E are enthusiastic they are often quite expressive, and there is little doubt about their enthusiasm. When people with a preference for I are enthusiastic, however, their enthusiasm is often more contained and, as a result, may not be so obvious to others.

This difference demonstrated itself several years ago when my partner Scott (having a preference for Introversion) and I (having a preference for Extraversion) were looking at buying a home together. One day we visited an open house for a place that had looked interesting to us online. Once we got there, however, we found ourselves lukewarm to its layout and unenthused about the amount of remodeling work that would be necessary to make it the home we wanted.

A few weeks later we were in that same neighborhood and noticed that there was an open house at the same place again. So just for kicks we decided to take a look at it one more time. There was a different realtor staffing the open house this time, and when we expressed our concern about the layout, he presented another idea for remodeling that was much more manageable and that addressed all of our concerns. I could feel myself bursting with excitement, but didn't want to tip off the agent about my interest any more than I already had, so we headed out to the car.

I could hardly wait until we were in the car. Once the doors were closed, I blurted out, "I think we should put an offer on it! If we did the remodeling that the realtor suggested, it would be a great house! I think we've found 'the one!' What do you think?"

Scott replied, "I think it's a good house."

"Oh," I said. "A 'good house?' What don't you like about it?"

"Nothing," he said, "I think it will be fine."

"Wait, 'fine?' If you don't like it, we shouldn't buy it. I want you

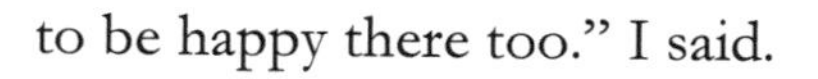

to be happy there too." I said.

"No, I think it will be good," he said.

And then I was reminded of our E and I differences.

"Oh, wait a minute!" I said. "Is this you being excited?!"

"Yes," he said.

And with our two forms of enthusiasm brimming both out and in, we agreed to put in an offer.

Oh, Was I Talking?

Another distinction between E's and I's is that E's usually like to talk things out in order to figure them out, and I's usually like to think things through in order to figure them out. In an MBTI workshop I conducted last year, this distinction caused some confusion to one participant, so during a break he called me over to his table.

"I've been wondering about my type," he said. "I thought I was an E, but now I'm not sure if I have a preference for E or I. I mean, sometimes I like to think things through, which is more like an I. But then other times I like to talk things out, which is more like an E. Like the other day at work, I had a problem I was trying to resolve on an employee issue, so I thought about it for a little while, but then I really needed to talk to one of my colleagues to figure out what to do, and that talking seemed to really help. And now that I mention it, I can see where a lot of times talking things out is really what I need to do…"

When I detected him taking a pause, I interjected, "Kind of like how you're talking it out right now?"

He laughed. "I think I just answered my own question!"

Exhibit A: Extraversion.

<u>Your Preference for E or I</u>

So you've just read some true type tales that describe E and I in real life.

Which one sounds more like you?

- ❑ **E**xtraversion

or

- ❑ **I**ntroversion

If you can't decide, read on to the next chapter. You can always come back to revisit E and I later!

Chapter 3
The Kind of Information You Like and Trust

The two opposites for this aspect of personality are "Sensing" and "Intuition." For this pair of opposites, we'll use the letters "S" for Sensing, and "N" for Intuition (since we already used "I" for Introversion). Let's take a look at the personality type descriptions for S and N, which address *the kind of information you like and trust*:

People with a preference for S:

- Like information that is tangle and verifiable
- Focus quickly on present realities and past experience
- Often describe themselves as practical and realistic people

- Need to understand the specifics first in order to understand the big picture

People with a preference for N:

- Like information that is abstract and conceptual
- Focus quickly on future possibilities and interpretations
- Often describe themselves as imaginative and "big picture" people
- Need to understand the big picture first in order to understand the specifics

Again, you'll probably see parts of yourself in both descriptions, since we all use both the Sensing and Intuition parts of ourselves. But the question you'll be trying to answer, like you just did with E and I, is not which one you *do*, but which one is your *natural preference.*

Before you decide, read the following S – N stories. As you read them, you'll likely find yourself identifying with one preference more than the other. Then at the end of this chapter, you'll have an opportunity to again select the preference that sounds most like you.

Signing Your Name

One day I was conducting an MBTI interpretation session via telephone with a client in Indiana. To illustrate the concept of personality preferences, I wanted to have her do the handwriting activity, just like the one you did at the beginning of this book.

So I said to her, "Please sign your name."

I had done this activity on the phone with scores of clients before, so was familiar with the timing. Usually it took about five or ten seconds for clients to sign their name, and when they finished they'd say, "OK, I'm done." That then became my cue to move forward.

With this particular client 10 seconds went by, then 15, then 20. And although I have a preference for Extraversion, I'm also trained as a counselor so I can sit in silence when it's part of my work. "Maybe she's very careful when she signs her name," I thought. But after 30 seconds, I was really beginning to wonder what was happening. Her name wasn't *that* long, after all!

And then I heard her say, "Hello?"

To which I replied, "Hello?"

And she said, "Are you there?"

And I said, "I'm here. Are *you* there?"

She said, "Yes, I'm here."

And I said, "Okay, good. Did you sign your name?"

And she said, "No, I didn't."

Slightly surprised, I replied, "Oh, why not?"

And she said, "Because you said, 'Sign your name,' and I don't know sign language."

"Oh!" I replied. "I meant your *signature*!" And we both had a good laugh.

Later in our session we learned that she has a preference for Sensing, and then the whole "signature" situation made perfect sense. We had encountered a classic Sensing – Intuition communication breakdown.

As a person with a preference for Intuition, I gave her a very general instruction: "Please sign your name." There wasn't any specific guideline or detail – even though it seemed crystal clear to me! In retrospect, however, I can see how that instruction could be vague or unclear to someone with a preference for Sensing. For example, I didn't say, "Please sign your signature as you normally would."

And as a person with a preference for Sensing, she took my

instruction very literally: "Sign your name." And because people with a preference for Sensing also tend to prize accuracy, she didn't want to misinterpret my instructions and do the wrong thing.

That is one of the incredible things about learning the language of personality type. Without it, I might have thought, "For crying out loud, quit being so literal." Or she might have thought, "This guy is pretty vague; I wonder if I'll get what I need in this session." But by knowing type, I could see that I needed to provide more Sensing information in our session – that is, specifics, facts, and practical applications of type – in order for our session to be a success. And it was!

Paying Attention

Scott and I recently took a trip to the Big Island of Hawaii to celebrate my birthday. On my birthday evening, we decided to treat ourselves to something special and had dinner at the restaurant at our resort. The restaurant was supposed to be one of the best on the island, and is on a grassy lawn right next to the Pacific Ocean. I was a little worried that it would be a little too stuffy or snooty for our tastes, so I was relieved when we were greeted by our friendly, laid-back waitress.

We soon learned that she had a wonderfully witty sense of humor that melded perfectly with ours. Throughout the night she spent quite a bit of time with us, which gave me an opportunity to be in my usual Extraverted "talk show host" mode and get to know her better. Soon we learned that she was in her early 60s, and that she had been on the Big Island for over 40 years. She was originally from Los Angeles and had been studying fashion design when she met a surfer and ran off to Hawaii. After arriving in Hawaii, she started waiting tables, and had been doing so ever since. She eventually married the surfer, but the marriage didn't last. She got divorced and then later remarried, this time to a cook at a restaurant at a different resort. They're wildly happy, and own two houses on the Big Island. They also own a third home in Mexico, where they plan to retire in two years.

The evening was an absolute delight – not only because of the amazing and innovative food or the incredible location, but also because of the great conversation with our waitress.

Later that evening, walking back to our room, we were recounting our dinner conversation and how enjoyable it had been.

"You know," I said to Scott, "This is a special trip, so what do you think about splurging and going back there for dinner tomorrow?"

"That's fine with me," he replied.

"OK, excellent. I'll call in the morning and make reservations," I said. "I'd really like to get that same waitress, though, because she was so great. The bummer is, I don't remember her name. But I can describe her and tell them she's the one who came from L.A. a long time ago and is married to a guy who cooks at the Mauna Kea resort. That should be enough for them to figure out who she is."

"Kit," Scott said.

"Kit what?" I replied.

"Her name is Kit," he said.

"How do you know that?" I asked in wonder.

He pointed to his chest. "Her name tag said 'Kit'."

"I hadn't even noticed," I replied.

And *that* is a perfect example of one of the many differences between people with a preference for Sensing and those with a preference for Intuition. He saw the data, I saw the theme.

Amazing.

Dollars for Details

As you just read in the last story, people with a preference for Sensing can usually remember a lot of details and specifics. And not only can they remember them, they tend to remember them *accurately*. Key detail.

It's not that people with a preference for Intuition can't remember a single detail or specific. It's just that their natural wiring predisposes them to remember details as they fit into the context of a theme, concept, or big picture idea, so the details are often secondary. Because the hardwiring of Sensing types predisposes them to focus on details and specifics *first*, S's naturally have a leg up in that department. As a result, when S's and N's compare the accuracy of their recollections, N's are often reminded that they may have remembered specifics, but they remembered them a little *wrong*.

I see examples of this difference between Sensing and Intuition frequently with two of my best friends in San Diego. Maria has a preference for Sensing, and her husband Angelo has a preference for Intuition. Often, when we are out for dinner together, they will be recounting a story of a recent trip they took or an event they attended together, and each one will remember things a bit differently. This was highlighted one night at dinner, when they were telling me about their recent trip to Las Vegas.

"We went to the art gallery at Bellagio," Maria said, "and we saw a really cool Andy Warhol exhibit. I had no idea he had done portraits of so many people."

Angelo added, "Yes, he did Jacqui Onassis, Elizabeth Taylor, Michael Jackson, Armani…"

"Oh, that wasn't Armani, honey, it was Versace," said Maria.

"No it wasn't, it was Armani," said Angelo.

"I think you have your designers mixed up. It was the third one down on the first wall of paintings. It was Versace, remember?" Maria said.

"I'll bet you a dollar!" said Angelo.

This has become the running joke with Angelo, Maria, and their friends – Angelo is always betting Maria a dollar when they don't agree on the accuracy of a particular fact.

After dinner we went back to their house for coffee. Determined to win his dollar, Angelo got onto the computer and went to the Bellagio website, and reviewed its description of the pieces in the Warhol exhibit. And sure enough, there it was. The piece in question was... Versace. And Maria once again became one dollar richer.

Now that's not to say that Angelo doesn't ever get one right or is sloppy with details. But let's just say... if you ever need change for a five, you might want to go to Maria!

<u>What's Your Reality?</u>

Another distinguishing factor between people with a preference for Sensing and people with a preference for Intuition is how they like to present information. People with a preference for S usually like to present information in a sequential order – "first this, then that." People with a preference for N usually like to present information by discussing the overall theme – "here's the big picture."

I saw this in black and white several years ago when a friend of mine from Southern California and another from New Zealand took international trips around the same time of the year. My Southern California friend took a trip to South Africa for work, and my New Zealand friend took her family on a trip to Europe. After their trips, they shared their travel experiences with their friends via email. One has a preference for Sensing, the other has a preference for Intuition.

Here's an excerpt of the email from my friend who has a

preference for Sensing:

The journey to Capetown began in Atlanta, Georgia, with me getting up at 4:30 am to finish packing. I arrived at the airport at 5:30 am, and had a couple of hours to kill, so had a cup of tea and a muffin, and then went online to do some banking. I also was able to get some South African currency, called Rand.

The flight was supposed to depart at 10:30 am, but it was 45 minutes late in leaving. I was back in steerage, in row 67 of 75 total downstairs in the 747. They fed us lunch shortly after takeoff, then dimmed the lights to acclimate us to South African time. It was 1:30 pm in Atlanta, but 8:30 pm in Capetown. The flight attendants came by frequently with water and juice, and gave us the little "kit" with slipper socks, an eyeshade, and toothbrush with toothpaste. I slept for several hours.

At 6:15 South Africa time they turned on the lights and served breakfast. The choice was pancakes or eggs; I had pancakes. I got into the bathroom to wash my face and brush my teeth, so felt pretty good when we were landing.

You can hear the sequential order of her story, and also the Sensing precision that includes times, seat numbers, and even aircraft type! I don't find this story boring at all. In fact, I can completely relate to what she experienced. Reading her email, I found myself thinking, "Oh, I know what it's like to be in airport for a couple of hours and to take care of some tasks online. And oh, I know exactly what she's talking about with the dimming of the cabin lights, and that little 'kit' that you get on an international flight." In fact, I felt like I was on the trip with her – sitting right next to her in seat 67B!

Now for contrast, here's an excerpt of the email from my friend who has a preference for Intuition:

Our trip to Europe was excellent. LOTS of inspiration, characters, pasta, pizza, red poppies, and the world's great explosion of artistic talent. Far out, what a time that must have been when those guys were creating one masterful, stunning thing after another. Wonder what I was – if I was around back then – the paint sniffer, or mixer, or posing as the daughter of a fabric merchant, while in the meantime I was secretly roaming around palaces in amazing red velvet, and hiding in one of the king's cupboards… if they had cupboards… I'd better check – I'll look it up under 'Top 10 Hiding Places When Spying For the Queen." Alas, I was probably stuck indoors learning manners or bodice stitching or whatever they did in those days."

Quite a difference! You can hear her interpretation of her experiences, and of all the images and feelings they brought up for her. I don't find this story "out there" at all. In fact, reading this one, I found myself thinking, "She's right, it must have been a very amazing time back then with all that creativity. And I can just picture her roaming around in red velvet, roaming around palaces…" I didn't, however, have a single clue about what countries she visited, or what museums she went to!

Both of these people described their travels *exactly* as they experienced them. What a trip.

Details, Details

Scott and I are big fans of the singer Adele. Before she became so well known, we had occasional conversations about the source of her accent. Neither of us was interested enough in the answer to research it, but periodically the topic would come up.

One day, after her first album was released, there was an online article about Adele and her new album. We read the article together, and after we finished, Scott said, "Well, at least now we know she's British."

Before I go any farther, I should remind you that I have a preference for Intuition. And despite that preference, I like to think that I am pretty good with details. In fact, one of the comments I hear from people about my work is, "You are so meticulous." However, for as good as I think I am with Sensing information, whenever I get around someone who has a natural preference for Sensing – like Scott – I am reminded of my S deficiencies. Now back to our story…

So I said to Scott, "How do we know she's British?"

And he said, "Read the first line of the article."

And there it was: "British pop star Adele…"

Once again, I never saw it. It was "Kit" revisited!

My Mind's Eye

Back in 2001 I decided to buy a house in San Diego. Since it was my second home purchase, I had some idea of what to expect. But unlike my first purchase, made at a time when the market was a buyer's market, this purchase was occurring at the beginning of the real estate frenzy in San Diego, and was definitely a seller's market. If you saw a house that you thought might even remotely be a possibility, you needed to put an offer in immediately, at or above the asking price.

I searched fruitlessly for several months, only to lose out on one house after another and to see home prices increase every week. One day my realtor called and said, "I think I've found the perfect house for you. Meet me there in an hour." So one hour later, I stood before a 1926 Craftsman cottage in a gentrifying neighborhood. One day later, I had an acceptance on my offer, and was awaiting the 60-day close of the sale.

In the first week after my offer had been accepted, I visited the home several times to get ideas about what I might do with the house once I owned it. It definitely needed some work. To give you an idea of what it was like, let me take you through a little tour of the home's condition.

The front yard hadn't been landscaped in years (and possibly decades), and consisted of dead grass and one, solitary, dying rose bush. The original wooden Craftsman front door, found in many of the neighboring houses, was gone, and had been replaced with a hollow-core closet door. The hardwood floors throughout the house were covered in carpet, and the hardwood floors in the kitchen had been covered over with new (and hideous) linoleum. The entire house was painted in a faded beige, giving the whole house a worn and tired look. The bathroom door was positioned so that when it was open, the living room and hallway were graced with a direct shot of the toilet. The bathroom floor was also covered with linoleum (even more hideous than the kitchen's), and the entire room was painted in a high-gloss faded peach. The bedrooms had venetian blinds that were covered in a thick film of dust mixed with years of cigarette smoke. They may have been white at one time, but not now. There was an addition off the back of the house, which I affectionately called "the knotty pine room." Everything in that room was knotty pine, except for the worn, gray, indoor-outdoor carpeting on the floor. The entire room was bathed in sickly green light, which came streaming in through the wavy-green-plexiglass overhang built off of the back of the house. Suffice it to say, the backyard was a disaster.

But I had a vision. And although I just described the original condition as it was, all I could see at the time was potential. That is one of the blessings – and curses – of having a preference for Intuition: You see potential in almost *everything*.

So one day I walked my friend Maria, who has a preference for Sensing, through the house. As we walked in the living room, I said, "Now picture that the carpet is gone and that the beautiful red oak hardwood floors underneath are refinished. And on either side of the fireplace, imagine the original drop-leaf desk and bookshelves are re-installed just like they were in 1926."

Then we went on to the bathroom. "This door is going to open in the opposite direction. And I'm going to take the floor out, and put in those little white and black hexagonal tiles like they had in the 1920s. This medicine cabinet is going to go, and I'll replace it with a wooden one and put Craftsman-style lights on either side. And the whole room will be white."

And so I continued, room by room, describing my vision for each one. When I finished the tour, I asked Maria, "So what do you think?"

And she said, "Don't you ever get overwhelmed by how much there is to do?"

There it was, one of the many differences between Sensing and Intuition. I had just taken her through "the house of the future," using my Intuition to describe all the possibilities I had envisioned. She, on the other hand, had seen "the house of the present," using her Sensing to focus on the reality of the home's actual condition.

Today, the vision of the house I had back then has been actualized. And now that I've finished restoring this house, I have my eye on buying another fixer.

Note to self: Take Maria through next house *before* buying.

Data and Stories

Earlier this year, I did an MBTI workshop for a group of physician leaders who were taking part in a year-long leadership development program. One of the activities I had them do involved having everyone with a preference for S form a group together, and everyone with a preference for N form a group together. Then I projected a picture from a children's book on the overhead screen and asked each group to simply look at it. After 15 seconds I blackened the screen and asked each group to discuss the picture. After 5 minutes of discussion, each group then reported out what they had discussed.

As you might expect, the group with a preference for Sensing saw and remembered a great amount of detail and specifics about the picture. They remembered exact placement ("In the lower left, there was a girl picking apples"), numbers of objects ("There were three rugs in the center of the picture"), and were careful not to make assumptions ("It looked like either a spider or a fly, but we couldn't tell for sure").

And as you might also expect, the group with a preference for Intuition saw and remembered a few specifics to begin with, and then gravitated toward patterns and interpretations. They assumed intention ("It looks like the spider was planning an attack on the little girl"), they hypothesized origin ("I wonder if it's from a fairy tale?"), and assigned meaning ("It's a metaphor for life – while you are going about your daily business, there is the unknown lurking right around the corner."). These differences prompted a great deal of discussion about how the S and N preferences impact their work.

One conversation centered around keeping patient records. There was much discussion around accuracy and thoroughness in making patient notes, which both the S's and N's agreed was important. The people with a preference for S noted that this kind of precise and detailed record keeping was quite easy for them to do. But then they turned to the group of N's and asked, "So how do you keep patient records if you don't focus on a lot of detail?"

The N's replied, "We include details because we know they're vital. But we put those details in the context of the patient's visit. We'll often start out by telling the 'story' about the patient and what happened during the appointment. That way the next person reading the chart has the full picture of what's going on."

"Oh!" replied the Sensing group. "NOW we know why certain files drive us crazy! We don't want the story first, we want the data first!"

And the N's replied, "But the data only make sense to us in relation to the story about what's happening with the patient!"

And the S's said, "And the story only makes sense to us if we first have the data to support it!"

Light bulbs were going off in the minds of both groups. They talked about the everyday event of an outgoing physician handing off patient records to an incoming physician during a shift change

-- and what a difference it would make and how much time it would save if the outgoing physician reviewed the records in a way that made sense to the incoming physician. If the incoming physician has a preference for S, then data first, story second; if the incoming physician has a preference for N, then story first, data second.

I've seen it be true time and time again: little changes like that can have a huge impact. That's data *and* a story I like.

Apples and Apples

Several years ago I conducted an MBTI team-building session with a group of mechanical engineers in San Diego. When it was time to do the Sensing-Intuition activity, I again had all the people with a preference for Sensing form one group, and all the people with a preference for Intuition form another group.

Instead of showing them the picture like I did in the last story, I decided this time to do something different. There was a basket of fruit in the room, and I took one green apple and one red apple and set them on the front table. I had each group look at the apples for 15 seconds, then removed the apples and asked each group to discuss the apples for five minutes.

In an activity like this, you would typically expect the Sensing group to describe the apples in rich detail and precision, citing size, color gradations, bruises, the existence or absence of stems, and similar concrete information. And you would expect the Intuition group to start off with a few details, and then move to patterns and connections, such as "It reminds me of apple pie," or "An apple a day keeps the doctor away."

After allowing 5 minutes of discussion in their groups, I debriefed each group. And as expected, the Sensing group described the apples in rich detail. "Just like clockwork," I thought to myself.

Then I debriefed the Intuition group, who… described the apples in rich detail! This can be a facilitator's worst nightmare, when the activities you do yield the complete opposite results that you expected. "Mayday, Mayday," I thought for a second.

But then I reminded myself, "You believe in personality differences, so don't panic. There's a reason why they've provided this answer, and your job is to uncover the reason and help them learn from it."

So I told the group of N's, "I have to tell you, your responses aren't what I expected from a group of N's! In fact, as you noticed, your responses were similar to those from the Sensing group. So I'm wondering, is there anyone in the group who thinks that maybe Intuition really isn't his or her true preference?" I thought that perhaps if someone was in the wrong group, that could explain the outcome. Not a single person raised a hand. "Rats." I thought.

Then I reminded myself, "Don't worry about having all the answers. Just ask good questions."

"Well let me ask you," I said to the Intuition group, "what do you think might have caused you to answer in more of a Sensing way?"

One of the engineers from the Intuition group said, "Well, first of all, we're mechanical engineers; we get *paid* to be Sensing. Second, we work for a parent company based in Scandinavia, and the corporate culture is very Sensing – you need to provide a lot of detail, be precise, and prove everything you do. We can do that, but at our core, we have a preference for Intuition, and it can get frustrating when we don't have a chance to create new things."

So this became a great example of how we all can use our less-preferred parts of ourselves, and we can even get good at using them – but it doesn't change those preferences from being *less-preferred* to *preferred.* And it also was a great example of how, if you don't get a chance to use your preferences in your work or life somehow, it can get frustrating.

Question answered. Facilitator relieved.

Literally

One of the characteristics of people with a preference for Sensing is that, because they are naturally attuned to realities, they often use straightforward language and use language literally. People with a preference for Intuition, however, are naturally attuned to interpretations, so they often like to play with language and will often use metaphors.

I saw a perfect example of this a couple of years ago when my friend Angelo and his wife Maria were hosting Maria's sister, Sheila, on her week-long visit from the Midwest. As a point of reference, Sheila has a preference for Sensing (more literal), and Angelo has a preference for Intuition (more metaphorical).

Over dinner, the subject came up about the number of visitors you get when you live in San Diego. This led to Angelo and Maria recounting all the guests they had hosted so far that year, and all the ones that were scheduled for the rest of the year. The number was quite large.

Angelo joked to Sheila, "Our house is so busy, it's like a bed and breakfast! And we haven't even had you sign the guest book yet!"

And Sheila replied, "There's a guest book?"

"No, I was just kidding," said Angelo.

"Weird joke," said Sheila.

OK, she didn't actually *say* that, but from the look on her face, I'm pretty sure she was *thinking* it.

So there was no guest book. And Sheila is no dummy. But it *was* a classic example of S-N communication.

Creativity

One of the biggest misconceptions about the Sensing and Intuition preferences is this: "People with a preference for Intuition are creative, and people with a preference for Sensing are not." And nothing could be farther from the truth!

I was first exposed to this mistaken notion in graduate school when doing research on the use of personality type in organizations. I found an article about a Fortune 500 company that used personality type extensively, and went so far as to create a special "Intuition Club" for those employees with a preference Intuition – because *clearly* the N's were the people who were going to have the vision for the future! Certainly those S's weren't thinking about the future; how could they, when all they were doing was taking in information from their five senses! *Groan.*

There are at least two problems with this "N's are creative, S's aren't" notion of creativity:

1) It assumes that if you have a preference for Intuition, you'll be good at it – and we know that isn't always the case. We've all seen examples of people who had lots of new ideas and visions – that turned out to be *bad* ideas and vision!

2) It confuses the *process* of creativity with the *product* of creativity. The *process* of how you create is influenced by your preference for S or N. But anyone can produce a creative *product*; they'll just create differently based on their preference for S or N.

When people with a preference for Sensing are creating something, they often begin by *starting* with what is known. They may likely look at what the specific goal is, understand the exact desired outcome, and then focus on what is currently being done and what has already been done in the past. People with a preference for Sensing aren't going to start creating something new until they understand what already exists. "Why reinvent the wheel?" is a motto you'll often hear from people with a preference for Sensing. Once they understand what "is," then they'll move into what "could be," adding in new ideas or new ways of doing things, and will end up with something new and creative. Do you hear the creative process of understanding the known first (Sensing), then adding in new ideas (Intuition), and creating something new?

When people with a preference for Intuition are creating something, they often begin by looking at a few realities, and then move quickly to future possibilities. They will likely look at the goal, spend a little time looking at what exists, and then use what exists to launch into imagining possible options or solutions. People with a preference for Intuition aren't going to spend much time on what's been done before or what already exists until they've had time to identify new possibilities. "Let's brainstorm!" is a motto you'll hear from people who have a preference for Intuition. Once they identify what "could be," they'll then look at what "is," seeing how the existing information fits with their new idea. Do you hear the creative process of identifying possibilities first (Intuition), then checking those possibilities against what already exists (Sensing), and creating something new?

Both types can end up with something creative; they just get there differently.

Here's an example. Let's say that I wanted to create a new brochure about my MBTI team-building workshops. If a group of people with a preference for Sensing took on this task, they'd likely begin by asking to see my existing brochure, and reviewing it thoroughly. They might also then obtain brochures from other organizations that offer similar team-building workshops to see what other brochures have included. Once they have gathered enough information about what exists, their Sensing preference will be satisfied. They'll then likely take the best content and ideas from the existing brochures, and then kick in their less-preferred Intuition preference to add in new ideas that no one included.

And the result? A creative brochure.

If a group of people with a preference for Intuition took on that same task, they may start out in a similar way by asking to see my existing brochure. They may even get a few brochures from other organizations offering similar trainings. But it won't be long before those brochures are tossed aside, and the group will start identifying new ways to present the information and new ways to put together the brochure. As they start creating options for the new brochure, their Intuition preference will be satisfied. Then they'll likely start referring back to the other brochures periodically, using their less-preferred Sensing preference to see what others have done, and then fitting anything good they find into their new brochure.

And the result? You guessed it! A creative brochure.

Taking Type to Work

Because I work with type every day, I tend to view the world through a type lens. A few years ago I was reading an article in a business magazine, and the Sensing and Intuition preferences jumped right off the page.

As some background for this story, it will be helpful to remember a few descriptors of Sensing types and Intuition types. People with a preference for Sensing tend to trust information that is tangible, factual, and verifiable. The Sensing motto is *"Prove it."* People with a preference for Intuition, on the other hand, tend to trust information that is intangible, conceptual, and abstract. The Intuition motto is *"Trust me."*

The article was written about a Product Designer who worked for a major appliance manufacturer. He wanted to make a change to an appliance that would have added $5 to the per-unit cost. The company's resource allocation team asked him to estimate the return on investment. In essence, they asked him to "prove it" –

the Sensing motto!

And doesn't that make sense, that a resource allocation team, which involves the allocation of money and resources – very Sensing things – would attract people with a preference for Sensing, which would then result in the request for proof?

Well, the Product Designer couldn't produce the numbers. The article then goes on to say that he fell back on the rationale of – and I'm not making this up, these were his exact words – *"Trust me. I'm a designer."* There it was – the N motto of "trust me!"

What we really have here, from a personality type perspective, is someone with a preference for Intuition, who has a "hunch" about a good design change, needing to somehow support his Intuition with some Sensing data in order to get the design change approved.

So as a solution, he created a standardized process that put design prototypes in front of customers. He gathered data about the customers' attraction to certain product features, and then compared those results against the results for their existing products and their competitor's products. This then gave him actual, tangible data to present to the resource allocation team. And they approved the design change.

This article didn't mention type directly once – but it mentioned type *indirectly* throughout the entire article! And as I read the article, I kept thinking how the designer's problem could have been addressed so much earlier had he known about type. Here's how:

If you have a preference for Intuition and are trying to influence someone who has a preference for Sensing, your Intuition ideas will get much more traction if you shore up your ideas with some Sensing information. Then, when you are presenting your ideas, *start* with the factual Sensing information, and then address how that Sensing information leads to your Intuition ideas.

And by the way, this concept works both ways. If you have a preference for Sensing and are trying to influence someone with a preference for Intuition, your Sensing information will get much more traction if you shore it up with some Intuition possibilities. Then, when you are presenting your information, *start* with the Intuition possibilities, and then address how those Intuition possibilities connect to the Sensing information.

So in short:

When you have a preference for Intuition, support your "Trust me" vision with "Prove it" information!

And when you have a preference for Sensing, support your "Prove it" information with "Trust Me" possibilities!

Showing Your Hand

Several years ago when conducting an MBTI workshop, I noticed a woman named Lois – who has a preference for Sensing – making a certain hand gesture when she spoke. After that, I started watching other people who have a preference for S to see if they made a similar gesture – and they did!

With that in mind, I started watching people who have a preference for Intuition to see if they made a different hand gesture when they spoke – and sure enough, they did!

Here's what I found:

Because people with a preference for Sensing like to explain information in sequential order, they make a hand gesture that reflects the sequencing of information as they speak. What they do is extend one hand, with all fingers pointing straight out, and then as they talk about information sequentially, they make a "chopping" gesture across the open palm of their other hand. It's as if they're chopping the sequence "1-2-3" across their other hand! It's what I initially called "The Lois Hand Chop," but now refer to more generally as the "Sensing Hand Chop."

And because people with a preference for Intuition like to explain information in a general, global way, they make a hand gesture that reflects the general nature of their explanations as they speak. What they do is take both of their hands, palm down, and put them side-by-side in front of their chest, and then as they talk about a big-picture concept, they arch each hand down simultaneously, the left hand down to the left, and the right hand down to the right. It's as if they're forming an arch that contains all the general thoughts they are communicating! It's what I refer to as the "Intuition Hand Arch."

Sometimes when I mention this in workshops people will laugh, but then say, "I don't think that's really true." And then sure enough, a little later, when people aren't paying attention to their hand gestures, someone who has a preference for Sensing will do the "Sensing Hand Chop," or someone who has a preference for Intuition will do the "Intuition Hand Arch."

And the hands don't lie!

Speaking a Foreign Language

I was born in France, and am always interested when people say, "The French are so rude." Now I'm not necessarily denying that people from my native land can be a little brusque at times. But I'm always curious what caused people to experience the French that way, so I'll often ask, "Oh, what makes you say that?"

And often they'll say, "Because they won't speak English."

And then there's the moment where we just stare at each other for a few seconds. And then I say, "Um, that's because they're *French*."

When you visit a country whose native language is different than your own, you soon learn an important lesson: You'll get a lot farther *faster* if you *start out* speaking that country's native language *before* you start speaking your own. And it usually doesn't matter how poorly you speak the other language; the "natives" immediately understand that you are at least trying to connect with them "where they live."

The same is true with the Sensing and Intuition preferences. It's natural for us to start speaking in the "type language" that matches our preference – which works great, as long as the recipient has that preference as well! But if you're speaking to someone with the opposite preference, your message can get lost.

However, if you *start* with the preference of the recipient, guess what? Just like speaking a foreign language, you'll get a lot farther faster.

There was a great example of this at an MBTI team building workshop I conducted last year for a healthcare company. We had just finished doing a Sensing-Intuition activity and people were still in their groups, one of people with a preference for Sensing and the other of people with a preference for Intuition. I wanted to take their newfound understanding of the S-N preferences and apply it to work so I said, "Now that you know who has a preference for Sensing and who has a preference for Intuition, take a look at your opposite group. Have you ever had a miscommunication with someone in the other group that you can now attribute to a difference between your preferences for S and N?"

And everyone in the room started murmuring.

"Hmmm…" I thought. "There's a juicy story here that everyone knows about."

"It sounds like there's an example," I said. "Would anyone be willing to share it?"

After some silence, finally one woman from the N group asked a colleague from the S group, "Should we just go ahead and bring it up?" And her colleague said, "Sure."

The "it" was a conflict the two recently had together when

working on a project. The project involved coming up with new ways of handling operations while complying with healthcare regulations, and the woman from the N group had been the project lead.

During one project meeting, the woman with a preference for Sensing arrived, bringing with her the hours and hours of regulatory research and analysis she had diligently assembled. She began presenting all the regulations in great detail to the N project lead.

After a few minutes of hearing the detailed presentation, the N said to the S, "Stop. This is way too much detail and way too much information. We're going to have to blow up this whole project and start over again." To which the S replied, as she pushed the regulations information across the table, "Good luck with that." And their meeting quickly adjourned. Several people in our workshop had been present in that meeting – hence the murmuring!

After hearing the story, I encouraged the two of them to take a few moments to reflect on their interaction, keeping in mind their preference differences for Sensing and Intuition.

I started with the woman with a preference for S. "What do you think you could you have said differently, now that you know your colleague has a preference for Intuition and needed to hear Intuition first?" I asked.

She replied, "I know what I wouldn't have done; I wouldn't have started out with so much detail. I think I would have tried to be more general. So I might have said, 'I know you're considering many different possibilities and options for this project. I think I have some information that can help us as we explore those different options.' And *then* I would have presented my research findings."

Then I asked the project lead with a preference for N, "And how would that have been for you?"

She said, "I think I would have been a lot more open since she started out with things that motivate my personality: possibilities and options. And she talked about how we could 'explore those different options,' which also seems much more general and open. I think then I would have been ready to hear, and actually interested in hearing, all of her information and analysis because I would have had a context for it."

One down, one to go.

So then I continued with the N leader. "You're not off the hook! Now that you know your colleague has a preference for Sensing, how could you have responded to her regulatory presentation – had she not started with the big picture and met your Intuition needs – besides saying, 'We're going to have to blow up this whole project?'"

She said, "I think I would have tried to acknowledge all the data she collected and the analysis she completed. I might have said something like, 'I can see that you've done a great deal of important research for this project, and I think it will be very useful. Can you give us the top 5 regulations that you think most impact this project?'"

Then I asked her S colleague, "How would that have been for you?"

And she replied, "At least I would have felt like my detailed research was valuable and useful. It might have taken me a few minutes to pick the top 5, because as an S, I like accuracy. But I could have done it. Knowing that my work was useful, I think I would have then been completely on board for exploring options."

A few months later, I was back at the same company doing another MBTI workshop. I ran into their VP of Human Resources and told her, "Remember that S-N example about the regulatory analysis? I talk about it every week in my workshops as a great example of how to use type."

And she said, "And you know what's really great? *We* talk about that example every week."

Excellent. That's a language everyone can understand.

<u>Your Preference for S or N</u>

So you've just read some true type tales of Sensing and Intuition.

Which one sounds more like you for this one?

- ☐ **S**ensing

or

- ☐ I**N**tuition

No worries if you can't decide. Just go on to the next one, and come back to S and N later!

Chapter 4
How You Make Decisions

This aspect of personality addresses how you make decisions, and the two opposites preferences are Thinking and Feeling. For these preferences, we'll use the letter "T" for Thinking, and "F" for Feeling. Let's take a look at the personality type descriptions for T and F, which address *how you make decisions:*

People with a preference for T:

- Like to make objective decisions
- Focus first on cause-and-effect when making decisions
- Naturally "step out" of a situation when making a decision, where they can be objective
- See people as one factor of many that affects a decision

- *Aren't* cold or uncaring decision-makers just because they have a preference for T

People with a preference for F:

- Like to make harmonious decisions
- Focus first on the impact on people when making decisions
- Naturally "step in" to a situation when making a decision, where they can put themselves in others' shoes
- See people as the primary factor that affects a decision
- *Aren't* emotional decision-makers just because they have a preference for F

Before you decide, read the following T – F stories. As with the other preferences you've already looked at, you'll likely find yourself identifying with one preference more than the other. At the end of this chapter, you'll also have an opportunity to select the preference that sounds most like you.

<u>You Like Me, You Really Like Me!</u>

As I mentioned in the E-I chapter, for many years I had great difficulty navigating my way through Canadian customs. After so many failed attempts to get through Canadian customs seamlessly, I was feeling especially nervous during a trip to Ottawa, Canada several years ago. Nervous – and determined to get through without a hitch.

By the way, as a point of reference for this story, I have a preference for Feeling decision making. As a result, I have a natural inclination to form relationships and to be relational, sometimes even with total strangers. You'll see why this is relevant in a few moments.

Upon landing, I made my way down to the Canadian customs area and dutifully waited in line. There were about ten customs kiosks in the area, with five customs officers on duty that day. As I drew near the front of the line, I began scanning back and forth to make sure I would be ready when an officer became available.

At the far left, there was a customs officer standing in front of a kiosk. I thought he must have been standing there to ensure that no one made illegal entry into Canada by sneaking down the walkway next to that kiosk.

He seemed like a nice enough guy, and I thought he must have been bored to tears. When he looked toward the line, I gave a quick and friendly "I'm not here to cause any trouble" smile.

When I got to the front of the line I began scanning even more feverishly for the next open kiosk. When I scanned left, I noticed that same officer, again looking toward the front of the line. "A little odd," I thought; but again, I gave a friendly smile, and continued scanning.

On my third glance in his direction, he then put his arms up in the air, as if to say, "Well, what are you waiting for?!" And at that moment, I realized that his kiosk was actually open, and he had been waiting for me to walk down.

This was not a good start.

When I arrived at his kiosk, he asked, "Were you going to stare at me all day?"

"Oh, I'm sorry, I didn't realize you were open," I said sheepishly.

And then things appeared to make a turn for the better when I thought I heard him say, "Welcome to Canada!"

Thinking to myself that this just confirmed that Canadians are amazingly friendly, I responded with an enthusiastic, "Thank you!"

Looking annoyed, he responded, "What?"

"Oh, I said thank you!" I repeated.

Awkward pause.

Then he said, tersely, "I'll repeat it again: WHY are you in Canada?"

Things were *not* getting better.

So my Feeling function had done it again. I guess we were really *not* going to be friends, and he had *not* been carting out the Canadian Welcome Wagon. He simply wanted to do his job and find out why I was there. Imagine!

Having learned my lesson not to Extravert my way through customs, I presented my paperwork that detailed that I was in Canada to conduct a four-day MBTI Certification Program for Canadians wishing to be trained on the instrument.

"Is that the personality test I took in Psychology class in college, the one that gave me a 4-letter personality type?" he asked.

Feeling that I might have finally pierced the armor, and that our emerging friendship was back on track, I replied, "Yes, exactly!"

I thought to myself, "Now surely I will sail through."

"I got an 'F' in that class," he said.

I couldn't even respond.

I don't know if he thought he had succeeded in wearing me down, or if I just had a look of resignation that said, "Either finish the job or send me on to the Immigration Office," but he stamped my documents and let me through.

There are so many lessons to learn. First, no Extraverting through customs. And now, no Feeling through customs!

Be My Guest

One of the most common misunderstandings between people with a preference for Thinking and people with a preference for Feeling is that T's can view F's as lacking in logic, and F's can view T's as unfeeling. I saw this very difference play out in a conversation I had with my friend Megan, who has a preference for Thinking.

The conversation took place shortly after I bought my first house in San Diego. In that house I finally had an extra room that I could use as a guest room. Up until that point, guests had stayed in a hide-a-bed in the living room, so I was quite excited about the prospect of giving them their own room and own space.

Megan, who lived on the East Coast at the time, was one of those frequent visitors. So one day we were on the phone discussing her next visit, and I told her, "I've got good news for you! When you come to visit, you'll finally get your own room. No more bar-across-the-back hide-a-bed!"

Megan said, "I never minded it, but that's great. I'll look forward to having my own guest suite."

Then I added, "Yes, it's going to be so nice to have that extra room for visitors. In fact, my sister and brother-in-law are coming out for a visit, and it will be great to give them their own room."

And then my F really kicked in. "But you know what?" I said, "My brother-in-law is kind of tall, and the bed in the guest room is only a full-size bed. Plus that room can get some street noise. I think what I'll do is have them stay in my room and I'll stay in the guest room. My bed's a lot bigger, the room is bigger, and they'll be more comfortable there."

In my way of thinking, *of course* I would put them in my room! As an F, I was putting myself in their shoes and thinking that putting them in my room would make them more comfortable. And putting my own needs aside wasn't an issue at all! It just seemed like the "right" thing to do.

After hearing this Megan responded, in logical T fashion, "Alternatively, they could stay in the guest room, and be glad that they have a free place to stay in San Diego."

I couldn't even respond. "What?" I thought to myself. It was like my brain got turned inside out with her comment, and I couldn't even process her line of thinking.

And then she threw in the kicker. "In fact," she said, "You don't know if having them stay in your room would make them *more* comfortable, or *less* comfortable."

At which point my brain exploded. Well, at least it *felt* that way!

"What?!" I said to myself again. "I thought I was making them *more* comfortable. I never even thought it could have the opposite effect!" Kaboom.

It really was amazing! She wasn't being mean, she wasn't being selfish, she wasn't being harsh; *my solution just didn't make logical sense to her.*

People often want to know the end of the story, and here's what happened: I put my sister and my brother-in-law in my room! But over time, I've learned to see Megan's logic. And also, I've had enough guests react uncomfortably when I've offered them my own room. So while my first reaction is still to accommodate, my T eventually kicks in. With Megan's help, I've learned to balance that F with some T logic. And my decisions are stronger because of it.

So now, if you ever come to visit me in San Diego… you're staying in the guest room!

Our "Relationship"

One characteristic of the Feeling preference is being acutely aware of others' emotions – or at least of what you *think* their emotions are! That very concept came up at a recent workshop.

During a T – F activity, the participants formed one group of people with a preference for Feeling, and another group of people with a preference for Thinking. The question they were to discuss in their groups was, "What about your opposites can impede communication?"

The group of F's discussed how difficult it was for them to be in a conversation with someone who appears to be mad – and that because T's often frown, they often appear mad. The F's went on to say that their natural inclination was to talk to the person about what was wrong. Once the "issue" was addressed, they said they could then proceed with the original conversation. But otherwise, for F's, leaving the "issue" unresolved was like having the proverbial two-ton elephant in the room.

The group of T's found this remarkable.

One T said, "When we're frowning, we're not mad. We're *thinking*. And remember, we're T's. If we're mad, we'll tell you."

Another T said, "This explains so much! Some of my F colleagues will come up to me and say, 'Are you mad at me?' And it's always so confusing to me, because I'm thinking, 'I'm not mad at you. In fact, I'm not having *any* feelings about you!'"

So for F's, a big learning is that not every interaction has a relational impact. And for T's, a big learning is how their natural style can have an unintended relational impact.

Our "Relationship" Continued

Several years ago I did a research study on personality type and conflict, and found that not only do T's and F's experience conflict differently, they even *define* it differently. For example, if you have a preference for T, an argument usually doesn't qualify as conflict; it's merely a discussion or debate. For T's the motto is, "It's nothing personal." If you have a preference for F, however, an argument often *is* seen as conflict. For F's the motto is, "It's *all* personal!"

This difference in viewpoint about conflict can often be seen in a meeting or conversation when a T and an F have a disagreement. Often there will be some back and forth, and perhaps some arguing and debating. Then the meeting and conversation ends, and the person who has a preference for T says:

"Want to grab lunch?"

And the person with a preference for F replies, "Not after what just happened."

And the T, looking perplexed, says, "What just happened?"

And the F replies, "We just had a *fight!*"

"A fight?" says the T. "I thought we were just having a discussion!"

I saw a real-life case of this during a training I conducted in Chicago several years ago. During the T-F portion of the training, I had the group form two groups, one of people with a preference for Thinking and another of people with a preference for Feeling. Each group was given the exact same conflict scenario to discuss, and after 10 minutes each group was to report out their response to the scenario. The intent of the activity was to illustrate the differences between the T and F decision making styles, with the T's taking a more objective approach, and the F's taking a more relational approach.

During their discussion I noticed that one person in the T group was sparring with the other people in that group. He was taking on the role of "Devil's Advocate," disagreeing with anything anyone said. As someone with a preference for F, I was tempted to step in and make things "right" (a.k.a. "harmonious) – but then I remembered, "They're T's; they'll work it out."

When the T group reported out their response to the conflict scenario to the entire group, one of the T's turned to the Devil's Advocate and said, in front of the whole group:

"I want to give you some feedback. When we were working on this activity, you seemed to take great satisfaction in negating any point that anyone raised. I'm all for finding holes in someone's logic, but you went beyond that."

A hush fell over the room. Again, I was tempted to mediate – was the Devil's Advocate okay? But then I remembered, "He's a T. He's probably taking the feedback objectively." And I let things unfold.

She continued on, "But actually you added little value to the conversation, and you need to be aware that your style of interaction can be ineffective."

The hush continued. After a few seconds of silence, I looked at the Devil's Advocate and asked him, "How are you doing right now?"

He looked at me, puzzled at the question. "I'm fine."

Then I looked at the T who had given him the feedback, and asked her, "How are you doing?"

And she responded, "I'm fine too."

Then I looked at the group of F's and asked them, "How are *you* doing?"

And they responded, "We're a wreck! We wanted to rush in and do an intervention!"

When actually, no intervention was necessary. Everything was just fine.

I Know How You Feel

Projection runs rampant in personality type. As I mentioned earlier, it's natural for each of us to take our own reactions to situations or events and assume that other people will have those same reactions to similar situations or events.

I suspected this was happening one night over dinner with a friend. She and I were discussing the house that Scott and I were considering buying in San Diego. The house had "good bones," as they say (translation: livable, but in need of major remodeling). Because Scott lives on the East Coast and I live in San Diego, I would naturally oversee much of the remodeling. And since Scott's relocation to San Diego was another couple of years off, most of the remodeling would be completed by the time he moved.

I was going over all of our remodeling ideas with my friend, which I found to be quite exciting. But then my friend (who has a preference for Feeling) said, "It makes me sad that when Scott moves out here, you'll already be in the house and most of the remodeling will be done. He's going to feel like he'll be moving into 'your' house, instead of you both moving into a house together."

I replied, "I think that's how *you'd* feel, but I'm pretty certain that's not how *Scott* would feel. Remember, you have a preference for Feeling and he has a preference for Thinking. I don't think he has that kind of emotion behind us moving into the house at the same time. In fact, I think he's quite happy that he doesn't have to be out here during the remodel! But you know what? I'll ask him when I talk to him tomorrow just to be sure."

So the next day I recounted the story to Scott. I didn't mention how I thought he'd respond, since I wanted him to answer candidly.

"So are you bummed out that we won't be moving into the house at the same time and working on the remodel together?" I asked.

"Can I be honest with you?" he asked. "I would be so glad to *not* be there during the remodel. You like that kind of thing, but it makes me nervous. I'd be happy to move into that house when it's all done."

So projection can happen when F's think that a situation that bothers them will also bother a T – when in fact, that situation might not bother the T at all!

By the way, the same projection can happen in the opposite way for T's. Something that might roll right off of a T's shoulder may actually hurt or offend an F – and the T might be surprised at the F's reaction. So T's may assume someone *isn't* feeling something, when that person actually *is*.

Tough Boys, Nice Girls

In many cultures, strong gender biases exist regarding the Thinking and Feeling preferences. In those cultures, men are often socialized and encouraged to be Thinking types – logical, analytical, and objective – and women are often socialized and encouraged to be Feeling types – compassionate, empathetic, and relational.

In those cultures, men who have a preference for Thinking usually don't experience much tension between their preference for T and what society encourages for their gender. Similarly, women who have a preference for Feeling usually don't experience much tension between their preference for F and what society encourages for their gender.

But what happens to female T's or male F's? For one thing, you may experience some tension between your natural personality preference and what society encourages for your gender. For example, if you're a female T, those glowing T descriptors of "logical, analytical, and objective" go out the window, and are often replaced by descriptors like "aggressive," "difficult," and usually some "b" words that include – but are not limited to – "bossy!" I can't tell you how many T women I've met who told me they grew up hearing, "Quit being so mean. That's not how nice girls act."

And if you're a male F, those glowing F descriptors of "compassionate, empathetic, and relational" go out the window, and are often replaced with descriptors like "too soft," "too weak," or "emotional." I can't tell you how many F males I've met who told me they grew up hearing, "Man up."

I think it's getting better, though. There are more T women who are role models in business, politics, and other settings that are making it equally desirable for women to be logical and tough. And there are more F men who are role models in entertainment and even sports that are making it equally desirable for men to be sensitive and relational. So there's hope!

I'm Just Trying to Help!

There's a common misperception that people with a preference for Thinking don't care about people, or don't care about helping them. Nothing could be farther from the truth!

What's funny is how different personality types demonstrate how they care about people and help them. People with a preference for T usually show they care about you by helping you logically solve your problems or improve your life. They're naturally wired to find the flaws and problems in situations or systems, and to identify logical solutions for making them right. They usually don't spend much time focusing on what's right, because "what's right" is already working. What's the point of focusing on that, when "what's wrong" is what needs fixing!

People who have a preference for F, on the other hand, usually show they care about you by helping you find the positive in whatever it is you're feeling or experiencing. They're naturally wired to focus on the relationships in situations or systems, and to identify outcomes that will please you and others. They'll spend quite a bit of time focusing on what's working well in a situation before they move on to what's wrong. In fact, sometimes the "what's wrong" can be so uncomfortable for them, they keep the focus on "what's right!"

These differences played out in my own life recently, when my friend Megan, who has a preference for T, came to me for some help. She had recently started a new job and was frustrated by the lack of competence in her new organization. She thought she was being underutilized, and she was bored. And as a T, Megan needed this problem to be fixed.

As someone with a preference for F, as I heard her story, here's what went through my mind: "Megan landed a great, high-paying job in the midst of a terrible economy. Her former company laid her off, but gave her a generous severance package, so she's been double-dipping two six-figure salaries for the past several months. Her new job moved her to the West Coast, which is where she wanted to be. She has so much to be thankful for, and she's not seeing it. I'll help her!"

Can you hear my gravitational pull to the Feeling preference – focusing on what's positive?

Now I always like to point out that, even as a type "expert" with over 20 years experience using and teaching others about personality type, sometimes my own type still gets in my way!

So what I said to Megan was, "You know what I think you should do? Volunteer in a cancer ward at a hospital. That might give you some perspective."

Translation: Focus on Feeling. Additional translation: "Focus on *my preference* for Feeling."

By the way, I believe that advice had its merits. But it's not what Megan needed to hear at the moment. She needed me to engage in logical analysis with her, not provide her with a lecture on being ungrateful. I would have gotten a lot farther if I had first *started* with the discussion of logical T solutions, like the possibility of her talking to her boss to identify an additional project or assignment on which she could be a contributor. And *then* I could have introduced my brilliant F "perspective adjusting" suggestion.

But instead, my suggestion was met with Megan's feedback: "That was NOT helpful."

Oopsie. My bad.

It also played out in the other direction, where I was the one who came to Megan for help. I was going through a rough patch in my relationship, and was telling Megan how I was becoming weary of the long-distance nature of my relationship. I was planning on bringing up the issue with Scott on an upcoming trip, as I wanted to have the conversation in person. But in the meantime, until the trip happened in two weeks, I was frustrated. I'm fairly certain what Megan heard was, "There must be a logical and objective way for Patrick to address this problem. I'll help him!"

So what Megan said was, "When you talk to Scott, approach it as a problem to solve, and work on finding a solution together. And try to stay objective."

Can you hear Megan's gravitational pull to Thinking – finding a logical solution?

And just like my advice had its merits, so did Megan's. But it's not what I needed to hear at the moment. I didn't need a logical solution; I needed some validation of my feelings. Had she started off with some kind of F statement, like, "That must be so hard, caring so much about someone and living so far apart," I would have been able to hear her logical T advice much more quickly.

But instead, I remember thinking, "Not helpful."

Oopsie. Her bad.

And here we were, both trying to be helpful! It's an ongoing process, remembering personality type and what different types need – versus giving them what *you* would need.

<u>You Say Tomato, and I Say Tomahto</u>

Since people with a preference for Feeling like to have harmony, conflict is usually not their favorite thing. In fact, they'll often find a way to bring harmony *into* a conflict situation. Often this happens when an F says in the midst of conflict, "I think we're really saying the same thing!"

To which people who have a preference for T, who don't find conflict as disorienting, will reply, "Actually, we're not."

I heard a variation of this in a recent workshop during a T-F activity. One of the F's said a phrase that we've all heard: "Well I guess we can just agree to disagree."

And one of the T's in the group said, "That phrase is so inaccurate. We're not agreeing *to* disagree; we're agreeing *that* we disagree!"

Do you hear the subtle difference? Agreeing *to* disagree puts the emphasis on the agreement; the end result is harmony! Agreeing *that* we disagree puts the emphasis on the disagreement; the end result is that harmony was actually not achieved!

One word can make a *big* difference.

Giving Feedback

The type concept of "T's focus on what needs fixing," and "F's focus on what's working well" also applies to giving feedback.

When providing feedback to someone at work, T's will naturally focus on what that person needs to improve upon. From the T perspective, what a person is already doing well doesn't need a lot of discussion, because those things are already working well – what *really* matters is what *isn't* working well and what needs improvement.

That kind of feedback can be effective when it's given from a T to another T, as they'll likely both be focused on what needs fixing. But when the recipient of the feedback has a preference for F, the feedback session may not be so effective! As the T points out what needs improvement – again, trying to make things better – the F, who has a preference to focus on what's working well, may only hear everything that is "wrong," and think, "Did I do ANYTHING well? Throw me a bone!"

Conversely, when providing feedback to someone at work, F's will naturally focus on what that person is doing well. From the F perspective, if that person needs improvement, why talk about that first – what *really* matters is validating what that person is already doing well!

Again, that kind of feedback can be effective when it's given from an F to another F, as they'll likely both be focused on what's working well. But when the recipient of the feedback has a preference for T, the feedback session may not be so effective! As the F is pointing out all the things the T does well – again, trying to help – the T, who has a preference to focus on what needs fixing, may only hear "fluff," and think, "When am I going to get some useful feedback? Get to the point!"

I've spoken with many T's who have said that, in order to be effective with F's at work, they've learned the "sandwich" approach to providing feedback. First, they start with F and say something "nice." Second, they get to T and say what they really wanted to say all along: What needs improvement! Third, they end with F and say something else "nice." When giving feedback to F's in this way, T's have discovered that the F "bread" can actually support the T "meat of the matter."

I've also spoken with many F's who've had to learn an opposite method in order to be effective with T's at work. They've learned that there are times when the F "bread" – that is, what's working well or what's positive – isn't needed or even helpful, and what they really need to focus on is the T "meat" – that is, what's not working well or what needs fixing. When giving feedback to T's in this way, F's have discovered that sometimes it's okay to skip the "bread" altogether.

T & F in Kids

People often ask when you can first see type preferences emerge in children. There are varying points of view on this, but I can tell you anecdotally that I noticed my niece and nephew's preferences for T and F when they were 3 and 5.

It first appeared to me when I was visiting my sister's family and witnessed an interaction between the kids. My niece, Delaney, smacked my nephew, Alex, in the arm. It was nothing malicious, just a smack in the arm. Alex seemed wounded – not physically, but relationally. It's like he thought, "Why would she do something so mean?" So my sister and her husband explained to Delaney why you don't hit people, and instructed her not to do it again.

So of course Delaney immediately smacked Alex again.

After my sister and her husband sent Delaney on a time out, I thought I would talk a little type with the two of them. They both knew their personality types: my sister has a preference for T, and my brother-in-law has a preference for F.

So I said to them, "I see some real type differences happening with the kids. It's not that Delaney is being mean-spirited or hurtful. But it seems to me that she might have a preference for T, and she wanted to objectively see the result of hitting her brother. The result was that Alex cried. It was like a lab experiment for her."

I continued, "And did you see how hurt Alex was that she would do such a thing? He is very sensitive, and it seems to me like he might have a preference for F. So after Delaney hit Alex the first time, she realized as a T that a sample of one incident isn't scientifically sound – so she hit him again. She was really conducting a test-retest reliability study! So it seems to me like a classic T-F interaction."

They were not amused, and told me to quit typing their children.

But my niece's preference for T and my nephew's preference for F became even clearer to me from a story my sister shared with me shortly thereafter.

My sister was driving the kids on errands around town in the family minivan. As they were driving, my niece, who was 4 at the time, started a conversation from her car seat in the back.

"Mommy," she said, "Sometimes I don't feel loved."

My sister (who, as you will recall, has a preference for T) said her first thought was, "Oh for crying out loud." But being a mother has helped her use her F preference more comfortably, so she responded with, "Is that so honey?"

"Yes," my niece replied. "Sometimes I feel like I don't belong in this family."

"I see," said my sister, remembering that the kids had watched a video the night before about a child who felt like a misfit in her family.

My niece continued, "Sometimes I feel I don't fit in."

My sister knew that she was a loving mother, and that she was in a loving relationship with her husband, and that they both showered their kids with love. And my sister was also very familiar with Delaney's behavior. Growing up, my sister was one to try and logically "test the system" in a variety of ways, and wasn't fragile when things didn't go her way – she wouldn't get sad, but she'd get mad that she hadn't been more clever at working the system.

And my sister thought this was one of those times when Delaney was doing the same thing. And my sister knew just the perfect response to the situation.

"Well honey," my sister started, "there's a good reason for that.

It's because you're really *not* part of this family. You see, you were born into a pack of wolves, but they couldn't keep you. So they dressed you in some tattered clothing, put you in a box, and left you on our front doorstep. The next morning when we went out to get the newspaper, there you were, so we took you in."

Now for some of you, that response might throw you right into therapy. And others might want to call Child Protective Services on my sister. But I assure you, she is a wonderful mother, and it really was the appropriate logical T response for my apparently-T niece!

Delaney burst into laughter. She was completely unfazed. She figured out that her strategy had not worked, and she found my sister's response funny.

My sister's response did not sit so well with my Feeling nephew, however. Alex was in his car seat, his bottom lip quivering, eyes welling with tears, saying to Delaney, "You were in tattered clothing…" He was having a full-on F response to the sad story he had just heard!

My sister, seeing he was upset, gave him the appropriate comforting, and told him it wasn't a real story and she was sorry she had made him upset. Alex was relieved.

I have continued to see these T and F differences with them into their adolescence. In fact, last summer when Alex was 13 and Delaney was 11, the three of us were driving around town when they asked me what my job was. I explained a little bit about people having different personalities, and how everyone has preferences for doing things in certain ways, and I helped people understand their preferences and what to do when other people have different preferences. I then thought I'd try and test my hypotheses about their preferences for T and F.

So I asked my nephew, "Hey Alex, how often do you get your feelings hurt by other people?"

And he said, "Oh Uncle Patrick, I get my feelings hurt all the time."

"One vote for F," I thought quietly to myself.

Then I asked my niece, "And Delaney, how often do you get your feelings hurt?"

"A lot," she said.

"Hmmm…" I thought, "Maybe I'm wrong about her preference for T after all."

"Well," she continued, "I don't really get hurt, but I get MAD."

"And there's one vote for T," I thought to myself.

We'll see if my hypotheses are correct when they get a bit older and I can give them the actual MBTI assessment. But I think I'm on the right track. Before I put this story in the book, I wanted to make sure the kids were okay with it so I had them read it first. Their feedback? Delaney liked that it made her sound clever. Alex liked that it made him sound sensitive. Hmmm… T and F?

T Humor

There's a thing called "T humor." It's the kind of humor that can have a bite to it, and when it's said by a T, it's funny – but when it's said by an F, it sounds nasty!

When I first started leading the MBTI Certification Program almost 15 years ago, I co-trained with a colleague who has a preference for T. I was delivering the portion of the program that had to do with the variety of MBTI reports that were available to produce. When I was talking about one especially lengthy report, I mentioned how the report's content was great, but that the report itself took a long time to print.

My colleague jumped in and said, "That wouldn't happen if you had a decent printer." The whole group laughed.

There was that T humor. My colleague thought it was funny, the group apparently found it humorous, but I, as an F, found it somewhat embarrassing – especially since she had recommended the exact printer I owned!

"Oh," I quickly replied, "You mean the printer that I just bought two months ago on your recommendation?"

And just when I thought the group would burst out in laughter a second time, I instead heard a collective, "Oooooooooh," as if I had just said fighting words.

"Wait a minute!" I said. "She gets laughter, and I get 'Oooooh'?!!' What's that about?"

And then they laughed.

But I got it. Her T humor was an objective statement with nothing personal meant by it. And there was no mistaking that my joke had an undercurrent with a personal "dig" in it.

So whenever I get that "Oooh" response to my humor, I know

that as an F, there's something I'm annoyed or upset about that I'm trying to disguise as a joke. And I'm a lot funnier if I just address the thing I'm annoyed or upset about – and *then* crack a joke.

The Book

One remarkable difference between T's and F's is how they define "fairness." In fact, you'll often hear T's and F's saying to each other, "I'm just trying to be fair!" The trick is, their definitions usually aren't the same.

For T's, "fairness" is often defined as "being consistent." T's will say that exceptions to being consistent can occur, but only if there is logic to support those exceptions. For F's, however, "fairness" is often defined as "considering the unique situations of individuals." F's will say that being consistent only makes sense when everyone's situation is identical – which, they will point out, rarely occurs.

This difference between T's and F's came up last year when I was doing a "Personality Type and Communication" workshop for a healthcare company. When we got to the portion of the workshop addressing T and F in communication, I had people form two groups based on their preference for either T or F. I then had them complete the statement, "When communicating with us, know that it's natural for us to…"

When the T group reported out their responses, they had statements you might expect from T's, like "Find flaws" and "Be objective." They also had the statement, "Play by the book."

Then I had the F group report out. They had statements you might expect from F's, like "Focus on the person" and "Validate the positive." And they also had the statement, "Play by the book."

Even though the groups worked at opposite ends of the room as they compiled their lists, they both had this one same comment!

So I asked the T group, "What does 'play by the book' mean to your group?"

And they responded, "It means we're going to be straight

shooters and consistent in our communication. Don't expect us to sugarcoat things that need to be said."

I then asked the F group, "And what does 'play by the book' mean to your group?"

And they responded, "It means we're going to take each person's needs into account as we communicate. We're going to be careful we don't hurt anyone's feelings as we communicate."

They were both playing by their respective books. The *contents* were just completely different! Once again, personality type shows us that two people can use the *exact same words*, and yet assign those words *completely* different meaning.

Outsourcing Feeling

It can be extremely helpful to have people in your life who have your opposite preferences. While each of us uses all eight personality preferences every day, we naturally gravitate toward our preferred preferences, and can overlook our opposite ones. That's when it's handy to have people in your life who have your opposite preferences – they can remind you to use your "other side," or can actually fill in those blanks for you. I call it "outsourcing your less-preferred preferences."

I've served this role with Scott, who has a preference for T. In the following story, I'm not so sure he actually "outsourced" his less-preferred preference of F to me, so much as I actually jumped in and took the job. But let's not quibble.

One year while we were on a vacation together, Scott got a call from his ex-wife, with whom he has a very good relationship. I could overhear the conversation, and apparently the prior evening their teenage daughter had been having stomach pains which had become worse overnight, so Scott's ex-wife had rushed their daughter to the emergency room.

As Scott was listening to the story, he periodically responded with "Okay" and "Alright." Part of that is due to his preference for T, so he keeps a cool head and stays logical, and part of it is his preference for Introversion, which makes him a man of few words.

I could continue to overhear the conversation (ok, so I was eavesdropping). Thankfully their daughter's condition turned out to be nothing serious, and she was sent home with some pain medication and was doing fine.

And again, Scott responded with "Okay" and "Alright."

As I was listening, I could hear the absence of any Feeling response on Scott's part. I had heard all that his ex-wife had done for their daughter – getting up in the middle of the night, schlepping her to the ER, sitting in the ER with her – and I could hear her getting agitated by hearing "Okay" and Alright." And while I knew that Scott was appreciative, he wasn't saying it.

I was sitting next to Scott as he was on the phone. Toward the end of their conversation, I started waving my arms to get his attention. He looked at me, quizzically.

I silently mouthed to him, "Thank you for everything you've done." He squinted his eyes like people do when they're confused. In retrospect, I'm sure he was thinking, "Why are you thanking me right now, and what did I do?" Again, he looked at me quizzically.

I then made the universal "telephone receiver" with my hand, holding my hand up to my face like I was talking on the phone, and pointed to the mouthpiece. And I mouthed to him again, but slower, "Thaaank yoooou for everythiiiing you've doooone."

Then his eyes got big, like people do when they've just figured something out. "Oh," he mouthed to me.

And then he said it. "Thank you for everything you've done. I really appreciate it." And what had been heading into a tense conversation, suddenly became a pleasant one.

Outsourcing Thinking

I, as a person with a preference for Feeling, have also found it extremely useful to outsource my less-preferred Thinking preference at times. One such time was over the summer when my neighbors had a birthday party for their 3-year old daughter. I'm not best friends with these neighbors by any stretch of the imagination, but we do talk when we see each other and bring each other up-to-date on what's happening in our lives.

It was a Sunday evening and I walked out to my back yard, when I heard a party happening in their back yard, complete with the "Happy Birthday" song being sung to their daughter. I found myself being hurt and somewhat incensed that I had not been invited. Never mind that attending a 3-year-old birthday party is not *anywhere* close to the top of my "Most Enjoyable Ways to Spend a Summer Sunday" list. And did I mention that we're not best friends? Well that's not the point. I had just seen them that morning, and surely they could have at least *mentioned* they were having a 3-year-old birthday party. By the way, don't try and find the logic. I admit, it's not there..

So I called Scott, who, as you will recall, has a preference for Thinking. I was going on about how I couldn't believe they didn't at least invite me and give me the opportunity to bow out (which, by the way, I suspect would have sent me into a separate whirlwind, probably involving guilt), and shouldn't you let your neighbors know you're having a party on a Sunday evening?

And with that last question, I opened up the outsourcing of my obviously overlooked Thinking preference.

So Scott, who was completely rational, said in his objective T way, "No, I don't think they should have to do that. They don't have to keep you informed of every social event they have, and they don't have to invite you to any of them either. And you don't really even want to be there anyway!"

Do you know how sometimes hearing another perspective just

makes you realize how absurd you were being? As soon as I heard his words, I just laughed. All that he just said was true. I had just worked myself into a frenzy over something I didn't even want. Now, upon reflection, I realized that what I *did* want was some affiliation with my neighbors, which I felt had been lacking – but making a production out of being allegedly "snubbed" from attending a three-year-old birthday party was probably a *bit* displaced. And Scott's objective Thinking preference helped me see that.

Later, Scott and I talked about what a good balance our preferences for T and F are for each other. Left to our own devices, who knows where we'd spin off to!

T-Spotting and F-Spotting

One cue that I referred to earlier is that T's will often frown when they are thinking. This can often be misinterpreted as disagreement, anger, or even downright dissention! And usually, it is just… *thinking*.

There's also a cue that F's give about their preference. When people who have a preference for Feeling are listening to someone talk, they will often mirror that person's affect or mood.

I just saw an example of this last week, when I met a colleague of mine for drinks. He used to live in San Diego, then moved to the Midwest for ten years, and had just moved back to San Diego. We hadn't been in touch for about a year, so we had a lot to catch up on. Here's how the conversation went – keeping in mind that I have a preference for Feeling:

"Hey, it is so great to see you!" I said enthusiastically. "How's the relocation been for you?"

"It is so great to be back!" he said. "I've missed living here, and it feels like coming back home. My wife and I found this great house that's five minutes from my work, so that's awesome. And you know I'm a runner, and I love running here. So all that's good."

"That is great!," I said, bursting with happiness for him – and mirroring his happiness. "And how is work?"

"Well, that's been a rough transition. I really loved what I did in my old job, but in order to get transferred here I had to make a job change. That's been really hard, since I'm not as crazy about what I'm doing now. The first few months I really wondered if I'd made the right decision."

"Oh, that's a drag," I said, mirroring the disappointment he had just expressed.

"Thanks. But now that I've gotten the hang of the new job, it's actually not so bad. What's been really hard is my relationship. My wife misses her family in the Midwest, she liked the job she used to have, and she misses where we used to live. We were having problems before we moved here, and now those problems are getting worse. It seems like we're really drifting apart."

"I am so sorry to hear that," I said, mirroring the sadness of his situation. "Are you in couple's therapy?"

"You know, that's what I've been thinking we should do," he replied. "We've been married for 8 years, and things only started getting shaky when we started talking about this move. She's a great person and we love each other so much. I think this move has been really stressful for both of us, and we've been so busy making it happen that we haven't taken very good care of our relationship. I'm going to talk to her tonight about getting some counseling and moving forward. And hey, thanks for that. I feel better just thinking about my wife and I working on this and working it out."

"No problem! I'm glad it helped!" I said, mirroring his newfound optimism.

For some people, and probably especially for people who have a preference for T, this kind of mirroring might seem exhausting! But for a person who has a preference for F, it's completely natural, and it satisfies the F hard-wiring to be emotionally connected with others.

So when you see someone mirroring your emotions in a story, you might strike up one point in favor of that person having a preference for Feeling!

Your Preference for T or F

Now you've just finished reading some true type tales about the Thinking and Feeling preferences.

Which one sounds more like you for this one?

- ❑ **T**hinking

or

- ❑ **F**eeling

If you're undecided on this one – well that would be ironic, since T and F *are* the decision-making preferences!

But again, no worries. Just read on to the next chapter, and come back to T and F later.

Chapter 5
How You Approach Life

The fourth aspect of personality addresses how you approach life, and the two opposites preferences are Judging and Perceiving. For these preferences we'll use the letter "J" for Judging and "P" for Perceiving. Let's take a look at the personality type descriptions for J and P, which address *how you approach life:*

People with a preference for J:

- Like having closure on things
- Get pleasure from making a plan and following it to get things finished
- Don't like a lot of last-minute changes, and may find them irritating

- Feel most comfortable when they're in control
- Are *not* "judgmental" just because they have a preference for J

People with a preference for P:

- Like keeping things open
- Get pleasure from starting things and seeing how they unfold
- Don't mind a lot of last-minute changes, and may find them energizing
- Feel most comfortable when they're going with the flow
- Do *not* have special powers of perception just because they have a preference for P

By now you know what to do next! Read on…

On Time

One of the characteristics of people who have a preference for Judging is that they usually like to get things done before those things are due – and they often expect others to do the same! Conversely, one of the characteristics of people who have a preference for Perceiving is that they often work with a flurry of activity right before something is due, and then get it done *just* in the nick of time.

As you might imagine, these differences can cause some tension and misunderstandings between J's and P's. In fact, you probably don't need to imagine it – you've probably experienced it firsthand! And in those times when those differences are ever-so-apparent, it can be *so* hard to remember that a person who has a completely opposite way of getting things done isn't trying to intentionally annoy you (usually, anyway!). They are just getting things done in a way that is as normal and natural for them as your way is for you.

This difference often emerges when I conduct workshops on personality type and conflict. In one such training in Vancouver, Canada, I had the participants break into two groups, one of people with a preference for J and one of people with a preference for P. In their groups, they had to come up with a list of responses to the question: "What about your opposites causes conflict for you?" There was no shortage of responses from either group.

When the J's debriefed their list, one of the items they brought up was this:

"You know what creates conflict for us when we're working with P's? We tell them that something is due at 5:00, and when do they get it to us? 4:58!"

All the J's nodded in agreement. I suspected that they secretly hoped their comments would help the P's see the error in their ways.

But the P's quickly responded:

"Which is technically two minutes early. So if you need something done at 4:57, just let us know!"

This brought down the house, and was a great learning for the J's. Being one myself, I took note.

<u>Taking Note</u>

In the last story I said I took note of the J-P learning from the conflict activity. But it appears that somehow I lost that note. Here's the story…

A couple of years ago I was contracted to conduct an MBTI team-building workshop at a large pharmaceutical company in Los Angeles. Because the workshop was being held in three weeks, I needed to give sufficient time for the team members to complete the MBTI personality assessment online, and also sufficient time for me to then download and print all their MBTI reports prior to the workshop. I sent an email to the team members with instructions for completing the assessment online, and set a due date of two weeks out, which was the Friday before the workshop.

Remember that thing about J's liking to finish things *well before* they're actually due, and expecting others to do the same? And remember that I have a preference for J?

Well as the two weeks progressed, one by one the team members completed their MBTI assessments online. And this was good news for me, since it was heading in the direction of meeting my unexpressed desire to have all their MBTI reports downloaded, printed, and ready-to-go well before the deadline! I started thinking I could have everything wrapped up at least one day before the deadline, and maybe even earlier. On the Thursday afternoon before the deadline, all the assessments were in – *but one.*

Oh, by the way, another useful piece of data about J's – they like *closure* and being able to check things off of their list.

So there I was, almost at the early finish line I had established, with my nose at the ribbon, but unable to push through because of this *one person.*

"What is taking her so long?" I wondered to myself, somewhat annoyed at this "delay."

Then I thought, "Maybe she's forgotten! I'll send her a simple little reminder just in case."

So I composed a quick email saying, "Just a reminder, you're MBTI assessment is due tomorrow by 5:00. Let me know if you have any questions!" I hit send, and could feel my nose pushing happily further against that finish line ribbon. Surely I'd receive her assessment results any moment!

Instead, a few minutes later I received the following email reply:

"I am well aware of that from your original instructions."

"Oh crap," I thought. "She's a P. And I just did my J thing to her."

I had communicated the deadline, she knew the deadline – but because she didn't get it done *early*, I treated her like she was late. And sure enough, when I downloaded her assessment results, she reported a preference for P. Groan.

The next week at the workshop when she received her MBTI report, she agreed with her P preference 100%. So at one point I pulled her aside and said, "About that email I sent you last Thursday. You knew all along what the deadline was, didn't you?"

And she said, "Sure did. I got it the first time."

So I said to her, as I've said before (and as I suspect I'll say again), "Dang, my J got in the way. I'm sorry about that."

Change Is Good

It's not that J's don't like change, it's just that they usually don't like last-minute changes to their plans. P's, in contrast, will often say that they don't find last-minute changes problematic, and in fact, they find them kind of exciting!

I have seen this often when I have gone out to dinner with my friends Angelo and Maria. Before we leave for dinner, we'll all discuss some options, and then eventually agree on a place that we all want to go to. Because Angelo and I both have a preference for J, we construe that agreement as a plan, and a plan to which everyone will of course adhere!

But for Maria, who has a preference for P, that agreement is merely a decision at that moment, and is *subject to change*.

So one evening we all decided to have Thai food, and were walking to the Thai restaurant we had all decided upon. Or, at least *Angelo and I* thought we all had decided upon.

But as we passed a new wine bar & restaurant, Maria said, "Oh, this looks really interesting, and I've read about this place! How about if we eat here instead?"

Now it's not that Angelo and I are rigid (that's our story and we're sticking to it). But we both said, "But we agreed we were having Thai food."

"I know," said Maria, "but I forgot about this place, and it's supposed to be really good. Why don't we give it a try?"

And this is what usually happens, and what happened that evening:

We give it a try, we have great fun, and Angelo and I are thankful that Maria made us shake up our routine a bit.

<u>Making Plans</u>

Because people with a preference for J like to have things planned out in advance, on Monday they usually have an idea of their upcoming weekend plans – and often for the weekends after that! And because people with a preference for P like to keep things open, they usually like to wait and see and keep their options open – even when it's actually the weekend!

This J-P difference demonstrated itself when I met Steve, who has a preference for P, at an MBTI workshop we both attended here in San Diego a few years ago. Steve and I had easy and fun conversations about type during the workshop, and thought it would be fun to get together to "talk type" over coffee sometime.

Over the next several months we met for coffee several times. Most of our coffee meetings happened when my phone would ring and Steve would be on the other end, saying, "I'm around the corner; do you want to meet for a quick cup of coffee?" And because I work from home and have a flexible schedule, I usually said "yes."

One day over coffee we discovered that we both liked biking along the bay. We agreed that we would get together and go for a ride sometime in the next few weeks. The following Tuesday, in true J fashion, I found myself thinking about my upcoming weekend plans. "This would be a great weekend to go bike riding with Steve!" I thought.

So I called him up, and said, "Hey, do you want to go for a bike ride on Saturday?"

And he replied, "I don't know; it's only Tuesday."

"Oh," I said, slightly disappointed. "I was hoping we could make plans."

"But I don't know what I'm going to want to do on Saturday yet, because it's only Tuesday," he responded.

"I understand that," I said, slightly lying. "But if we don't make plans now, something else might come up for me on Saturday morning, and then we won't be able to go."

"If something else comes up," he said, "then go ahead and do it. And we'll go some other time. Why don't we check in on Saturday morning?"

"Well, because I was kind of hoping to put it in my calendar," I said, realizing our J-P differences were in prime form. "But I think we've just encountered the classic J-P dilemma, haven't we?"

"I think we have," he replied.

So I compromised and waited. But not all the way until Saturday morning! I was still a J after all – so I called Friday night. And he compromised and committed to going, and we had a great time bike riding the next day.

And *that* is how J and P work at their best.

The Last Minute

Earlier this year I was preparing to do an MBTI workshop for a company in Northern California. I had been working with my contact there, Bob, who has a preference for J. Bob was handling some of the logistics for the workshop, such as procuring equipment for the training room and making sure the room had adequate supplies. This was Bob's first experience coordinating a workshop of this kind, so it was all new to him.

A week before the workshop, I received an email from Bob with the subject, "Last Minute Details." In the email, Bob asked how I wanted the participant names to appear on the name cards, and if I was available for dinner the night before the workshop. He wrote, "I'm learning about all of the last-minute details that go into a workshop like this!"

I laughed when I read this! I wrote back to Bob and said, "Only someone with a preference for J would say that 'the last minute' was one week before the workshop!"

During the workshop, when we discussed the differences between J and P, Bob shared the story of his "last minute" email with the group. The P's in the group roared with laughter, while the J's were trying to figure out what was so funny. In their view, Bob *had* been working "at the last minute!"

And the P's said, "Oh no, you see for us, the 'last minute' is usually just that: literally, *the last minute!*"

Packing

Earlier this year, two friends of mine – one with a preference for J, and one with a preference for P – went on a vacation to Africa together. When they returned to San Diego and shared their vacation photos with me, two photos jumped out at me as perfect examples of the differences between someone with a preference for J and someone with a preference for P.

The photos are on the next page; see if you can spot which one is the J and which one is the P!

J or P?

J or P??

In case you couldn't tell, the first photo was of my friend who has a preference for J, and the second photo is of my friend who has a preference for P.

And just for the record, my J friend wanted me to make sure you know that she is not "anal!" And my P friend wanted me to make sure you know that she found everything she needed just fine.

So now you know. Which means as a J, I can now check their requests off of *my* list!

Speaking of Lists

There's a common misconception that J's are the list makers and P's are not. The truth is, both are list-makers, but they make different *kinds* of lists.

People with a preference for J usually make lists for every day, and those lists typically have bulleted or numbered items of things to get done. And for those of you who are J's, you know there are few sensations in the world that are quite as good as crossing something off of your to-do list. In fact, J's like crossing things off of their lists so much that when they do something that wasn't on their list, they'll add it – and immediately cross it off!

People with a preference for P, on the other hand, make lists of things to do… someday. Those can be things to do today, tomorrow, next week, after retirement – but they all get put on the list. Sometimes P's also say they keep multiple lists in multiple places. And P's will usually say that it's the *making* of the list that they enjoy and that they find useful – more than crossing things off the list, or even finding it, for that matter.

My friend Patti has a preference for P, and one day when I was at her house, I spotted her to-do list. "THIS is your to-do list?!" I asked.

"Yes, it keeps me organized!" she responded.

Realizing I had just found a perfect example of a P list, I exclaimed, "OK, I'm taking this and using it in a workshop!"

Now if you took my list away from me, as a J, I'd completely flounder. But Patti's response?

"OK, no problem. I have others," she laughed.

Continuing to Talk About Lists

Here is the list I stole from my friend Patti (who by the way, wants to be sure you know that she gets things done!):

And just for contrast, here is one of my lists:

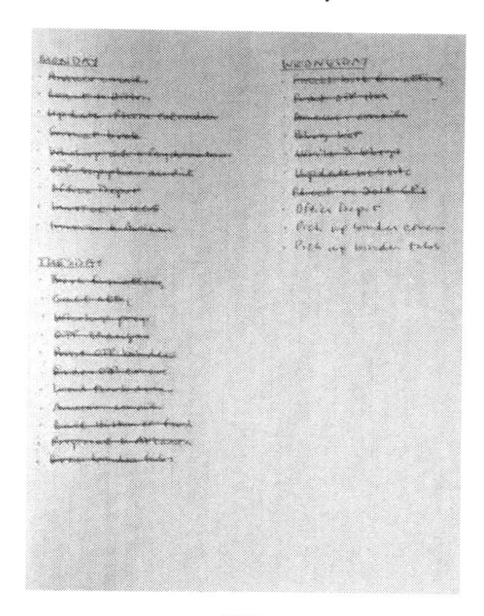

To be quite honest, I am somewhat horrified that several items on my list weren't crossed off. How embarrassing!

<u>It's a Plan</u>

Here's another great story about my friend Patti, who has a preference for P.

Patti's husband's birthday is on June 6th. One year, on May 11th, I was at their house, and Patti and I were talking about her husband's upcoming birthday. Since his birthday was rapidly approaching – "rapidly" in my J brain, at least – I wondered what she had in mind to celebrate.

So I asked Patti, "What do you have planned to celebrate Danny's birthday?"

And she replied, "I have no idea. It's only May, and his birthday isn't until June 6th! I'll have a better idea at the beginning of June…"

The J motto? "There's nothing like a good plan." And the P motto? "There's nothing like a good rush!"

<u>You're Doing It Wrong</u>

Last year at one of my MBTI team-building workshops, a participant came up to talk to me at the break. "I need to talk to you about my son," he said.

"OK," I replied, "What's going on?"

"He's a junior in high school, and he's driving me crazy!" he said.

My inside voice said, "He's a junior in high school. His job *is* to drive you crazy!" But my outside voice said, "Why is he driving you crazy?"

"When he works on a school project or writes a paper, he always waits until the last minute," he said. "I keep telling him he needs to plan ahead and start early, but he doesn't listen! It's always wait, wait, wait, and then he works non-stop and into the night."

"Does he get his assignments done?" I asked.

"Yes," he replied.

"And how are his grades?" I inquired.

"He has a 3.9 GPA," he replied.

"Are you pleased with his grades?" I asked.

"Yes, he's doing well," he replied.

"And what's your preference – J or P?" I asked.

"I'm a J. But what should I do with my son?" he begged.

"Give him a break!" I said with a smile. "He's got a system that works, and it's producing excellent results. It sounds like he might be a P, and P's do their best work under the pressure of a deadline. In fact, if they start early like J's do, they actually produce worse results! If he ever drops the ball, or his grades slip, then you have a performance issue. But right now, all I hear is a preference issue."

"I was afraid you'd say that!" he said. But I could tell, he got it. And kudos to him for asking the question to begin with.

Your Preference for J or P

This is your last one to decide on! And if you have a preference for J, that may give you a great sense of closure, because now we've worked through all four preferences. And if you have a preference for P, finishing all four preferences may be a little disappointing! But not to worry; there's still a bit more after this.

So which one sounds more like you for J and P?

❑ **J**udging

or

❑ **P**erceiving

If this one's not clear for you, that's fine. You can come back to it later to decide. For now, you can move on to the next chapter.

Chapter 6
What Are Your Personality Preferences?

Now that you've finished reading stories about each of the aspects of personality type, let's take a look at what all four of your preferences are. On the next page, circle whichever preference sounds most like you in each pair. If you're not sure about any of the preferences, that's fine. Figuring out your type preferences can take some reflection, so give yourself some time. You can always come back to that page later.

From page 79:

E (Extraversion)	or	**I** (Introversion)

From page 141:

S (Sensing)	or	**N** (Intuition)

From page 209:

T (Thinking)	or	**F** (Feeling)

From page 243:

J (Judging)	or	**P** (Perceiving)

As you've seen throughout this book, you can get a lot of practical use and insight from knowing your four personality preferences and what they mean. And even if you forget your four letters, you can still use type! I recently had a great example of just that.

I was having a conversation with a physician who had taken one of my MBTI leadership workshops and wanted to bring me into her medical group to do personality type work with her own team. She mentioned the MBTI workshop to her team, and one team member who was skeptical about type said, "I've done it before, but can never remember my four letters. I think we should do something else." The physician asked me how I would respond to that.

Since the physician had attended one of my type workshops, I asked her:

"Forget about your four letters for a minute. What do you

remember about your personality?"

She said, "Well, I know I like to talk things out, and I have to watch that I don't talk too much in meetings. I can get pretty specific about things, and sometimes I lose the big picture. I'm really concerned about how people feel, which is good, but I also need to make sure I don't over-personalize things. And I know I'm totally spontaneous, which can drive some people crazy."

"Perfect!" I said. "Learning about your four preferences in the workshop several months ago helped you figure all that out, and also helped you figure out that there are people who are wired to do things in the exact opposite way. And you just described your four preferences – E, with talking in meetings; S, with focusing on specifics; F, with concern about people; and P, with being spontaneous. Now if you could remember your four letters that would be great, and would make it easier to have type-related conversations with your team. But what's even more important is that you remembered what your four letters *mean* and how to use that information in your work. And isn't that what really matters?" And we did the workshop for her team.

So to make the best and most manageable use of personality preferences in your own life, keep it simple:

1) Understand your own four preferences
2) Understand your opposite four preferences
3) Learn how to use your knowledge of the eight personality preferences in your everyday life.

Then, as you become more fluent with your understanding of all eight preferences, you can "take it up a notch" and start learning more about the different combinations of preferences and what they mean. There are descriptions for combining all four letters together, combining the middle two letters, combining the first and last letters, and more. And while that information can be interesting and even useful – unless you consistently use type in your life every day, it can also be quickly forgotten. So for now, let's get the best use of the fundamentals of type. We can keep the complex stuff for my *next* book!

Chapter 7
Using Personality Type in Your Everyday Life

It would be so much simpler if everyone wore a lapel pin with his or her four preferences on it! That way you could read a person's type preferences, think about the best way to communicate with that person, and then adjust your style accordingly.

In the absence of that information, however, we can still make good use of type when we're interacting with people whose type we don't know. And we can do that by learning how to pick up on the "type cues" they give us.

I'll give you a great example of how that works. Last year, I did an individual MBTI interpretation session with Donna. Donna and her husband, Tom, co-own two optical centers.

After working with me and understanding her own personality preferences, Donna thought that an MBTI workshop would be useful for their entire optician staff and support staff so that they could better understand themselves, each other, and their clients. Since she co-owned the business with Tom, however, she needed his buy-in.

Several months after my work with Donna, she and Tom were in San Diego for an optician's conference. Donna thought this would be a good time for me to meet Tom, and to explain to him the benefits of an MBTI workshop. I didn't know Tom's type preferences, but I had my antennae up to pick up on any type cues he might send out.

When we all arrived at the restaurant, Tom and I shook hands, and Tom didn't say much. Then Donna and I (both of whom have a preference for E) started chatting about their trip, what they had seen around San Diego, and how the conference was going. Tom listened in on the conversation, and after a few minutes said, "Should we sit down and get started?"

"One vote for Introversion," I thought to myself.

When we sat down, Donna and I engaged in some more small talk. Then Tom said, "Let's get straight to business. Donna found the MBTI assessment to be very useful. In addition, one of our opticians uses her knowledge of personality type when she's working with clients, and she's our top-selling optician as a result. And the bottom line is, we are in the business of selling frames and lenses. Yes, we're in the helping business, but if we don't sell frames and lenses, we don't have a business. We have seven other opticians, and I want them to increase their sales too. So I want to hear about other similar organizations you've done MBTI workshops with, what you did with them in those workshops, and how those workshops increased their sales."

So right away, in my type-oriented brain, I tried to pick up on some of Tom's type cues. Here's what I came up with:

- E or I? I had already guessed his preference for **Introversion**, since he didn't engage in small talk, and chose his words carefully.

- S or N? For his second letter, I guessed **Sensing**, because he was very precise in his language, and focused on specifics, like "seven opticians." Plus, Tom wanted me to prove the effectiveness of my MBTI work by hearing about specific past workshops.

- T or F? For his third letter, I guessed **Thinking**. Tom was not building a personal relationship with me or trying to be my friend. It was all business.

- J or P? And for his last letter, I guessed **Judging**. He was very organized in his delivery, and was focused on an outcome, not an exploration.

Since my preferences are for E, N, F, and J, this meant that three of our four preferences were different. This was useful data for me!

Before I go on to the next part of the story, let's take a look at a list of type cues for each of the eight preferences. You'll find that these cues will help you understand each preference even better, and will also increase your ability to recognize type cues in your own everyday interactions.

As you read the lists of cues on the following pages, think of someone you interact with frequently. Can you spot any of the type cues that person sends out?

E (Extraversion) Cues:

- ❑ Strikes up small talk
- ❑ Interacts with many people
- ❑ Focuses on several people or activities while interacting
- ❑ Talks freely, and about a breadth of topics
- ❑ Appears enthusiastic & animated
- ❑ Adds on to, interrupts, or finishes other people's sentences

I (Introversion) Cues:

- ❑ Dislikes small talk
- ❑ Interacts with a few people
- ❑ Focuses on one person at a time when interacting
- ❑ Talks sparingly – or in great depth about one topic
- ❑ Appears calm & reserved
- ❑ Waits until others are finished speaking before responding

S (Sensing) Cues:

- ❑ Focuses on and asks for facts and details
- ❑ Talks about specifics before discussing possible options
- ❑ Uses specific, literal language
- ❑ Expresses thoughts sequentially, e.g. "First this, then that…"
- ❑ Does the "Sensing Hand Chop" (see page 129)
- ❑ Asks you to back up if steps are skipped

N (Intuition) Cues:

- ❑ Focuses on and asks for the big picture
- ❑ Talks about possible options before discussing specifics
- ❑ Uses metaphors and analogies
- ❑ Expresses thoughts generally, e.g. "So overall,…"
- ❑ Does the "Intuition Hand Arch" (see page 130)
- ❑ Doesn't mind if steps are skipped, as long as the big picture is addressed

T (Thinking) Cues:

- ❑ Is direct and to the point
- ❑ Speaks objectively, e.g. "I think…"
- ❑ Builds the relationship by focusing on the problem
- ❑ Looks for flaws and expresses disagreement candidly
- ❑ Appears businesslike
- ❑ Tests other peoples' knowledge

F (Feeling) Cues:

- ❑ "Feels out" other people to get a sense of how to proceed
- ❑ Speaks personally, e.g. "I feel…"
- ❑ Builds the relationship by focusing on the person
- ❑ Looks for what's right and expresses disagreement gently
- ❑ Appears warm & friendly
- ❑ Accepts other peoples' knowledge

J (Judging) Cues:

- ❑ Makes decisions quickly, sometimes prematurely
- ❑ Uses one checklist
- ❑ Likes an organized approach
- ❑ Is early for meetings
- ❑ Uses "…ed" words, e.g. "I've decided to…"
- ❑ Has a hurried pace, watching the time

P (Perceiving) Cues:

- ❑ Postpones decisions, sometimes until the last minute
- ❑ Uses several lists
- ❑ Likes an exploratory approach
- ❑ Arrives for meetings "just in time"
- ❑ Uses "…ing" words, e.g. "I'm considering…"
- ❑ Has a relaxed pace, enjoying the process

By the way, it's important to remember that when we're trying to pick up on type cues from a person, we can't always be certain that those cues reflect that person's actual personality preferences. Occasionally you might be picking up on a cue that relates to something *besides* a person's true personality preferences, such as what that person has been trained to do or what that person's culture or family has encouraged. But those cues still provide us with valuable information about what that person is "putting out there," what they need or want, and how we might best respond.

It's one thing to recognize the type cues that people send off – but that's only half the story! The other half is to "flex your style," especially if you find you are communicating with someone whose preferences are different from yours.

Let's continue with my story about Tom. Having picked up on his type cues of I, S, T, and J, I made the following adjustments to my usual E, N, F, and J presentation style:

- E → I: Instead of Extraverting and talking my ideas out, I tried to use my words economically, and to allow for introverted quiet time in between my statements.

- N → S: Rather than talking about the big picture or telling him, "Trust me, I've done this a thousand times before and it's always been great," I was very specific. I described the exact content of three prior sales-related type workshops I had conducted, specified the measurable outcomes that resulted from each workshop, and identified the realistic outcomes he could expect from our workshop.

- F → T: Instead of using my usual Feeling style, which would have been trying to make a personal connection with Tom, I kept it all business and objective.

Thank goodness I could use my natural Judging preference, and be planful and outcome-oriented!

When I finished, there was a pause. And then Tom said:

"This sounds great. Let's book some dates."

Whew! I had done it! I had picked up on his type cues, flexed my style to meet what I thought were his preferences, and seem to have spoken his language successfully.

Several months later when I conducted the MBTI workshop for the opticians and the staff, Tom received his MBTI report. He reported I, S, T, and J on the MBTI instrument, and verified that those were indeed his type preferences. After the workshop, Donna, Tom, and I went out for dinner to celebrate the success of the workshop. I recounted my story to Tom about first meeting him, picking up on his type cues, and adjusting my style accordingly.

"And it's a good thing you did," said Tom, "because if you hadn't, and you had talked a lot, been conceptual and only focused on people, we wouldn't be sitting here right now." Translation: "If you'd only used your E, N, and F preferences, we wouldn't be sitting here right now."

So picking up on type cues and flexing your style can be quite powerful – and it can pay off!

To help you flex your type style, on the following pages are lists of tips and suggestions for communicating more effectively with each of the eight preferences. As you read these tips and suggestions, think of the person you identified earlier. Are you flexing your type style when you interact with that person?

When they have a preference for E (Extraversion):

- [ ] Introduce yourself, and make a comment about the weather, their clothing, etc.
- [ ] Let them talk
- [ ] Reply back quickly with a verbal or non-verbal cue to let them know you're engaged in the conversation (e.g., "Oh, I see…" or a head-nod)
- [ ] Keep the conversation moving and ask questions
- [ ] If you need time to think or formulate a response, say so out loud
- [ ] Don't be concerned about editing your thoughts. Remember, E's think out loud, so they won't hold you to everything you say!

▶ **If you both have a preference for E,** watch that you don't get too loud or animated! Use Introversion to ask, "Could we benefit from some quiet time or reflection?"

When they have a preference for I (Introversion):

- ❑ Keep small talk to a minimum
- ❑ Wait for them to respond; don't fill the space
- ❑ Slow down, and don't reply too quickly or interrupt with comments such as, "Yes, I agree"
- ❑ Focus on them, and don't get distracted
- ❑ If you need to think out loud, let them know
- ❑ Edit your thoughts before you say them. Remember, I's process internally, so they'll expect that what you say has been somewhat "polished" already!

▶ **If you both have a preference for I,** watch that you don't operate in a vacuum! Use Extraversion to ask, "Could we benefit from some discussion with others?"

When they have a preference for S (Sensing):

- ❑ Be specific about the topic you're discussing
- ❑ Walk through procedures or processes step-by-step
- ❑ Provide specific examples and real, immediate applications
- ❑ Have relevant facts and information ready, along with useful written materials
- ❑ Try to minimize analogies or other abstract language
- ❑ Don't change topics rapidly. Remember, S's like to understand one topic thoroughly before moving on to the next!

▶ **If you both have a preference for S,** watch that you don't get too granular! Use Intuition to ask, "What are some other possibilities?"

When they have a preference for N (Intuition):

- ❑ Talk about the general theme you're discussing
- ❑ Provide an overview first, then talk briefly about steps
- ❑ Discuss and entertain possibilities, even if they seem far-fetched
- ❑ Don't give them too many facts or too many materials right away
- ❑ Try to use analogies and metaphors
- ❑ Don't be concerned about staying on one topic before moving to the next. Remember, N's like to get the "gist" of things!

▶ **If you both have a preference for N,** watch that you don't get too far out there! Use Sensing to ask, "Is this practical?"

When they have a preference for T (Thinking):

- ❑ Be direct and to the point
- ❑ Demonstrate or articulate your professional competence and experience
- ❑ Discuss pros and cons
- ❑ Don't sugarcoat or overlook negative or "uncomfortable" issues
- ❑ Conduct the relationship in a businesslike way
- ❑ Don't take their critical feedback or disagreement personally. Remember, for T's, it's about the subject, not the person!

▶ **If you both have a preference for T,** watch that you don't overdo the logic! Use Feeling to ask, "How might people feel about this?"

When they have a preference for F (Feeling):

- ❑ Be friendly and personal
- ❑ Demonstrate your interpersonal competence by showing that you care about them as a person
- ❑ Ask about what's important to them and what they value
- ❑ Mention what's right, or focus on areas of agreement first; soften negative issues
- ❑ Conduct the relationship personally, showing warmth
- ❑ Be cautious about how you disagree or provide feedback. Remember, for F's, it's all about the relationship!

▶ **If you both have a preference for F,** watch that you don't get overly people-focused! Use Thinking to ask, "What are the possible flaws?"

When they have a preference for J (Judging):

- ❑ Arrive early and finish early if possible
- ❑ Focus on organizing the interaction
- ❑ Try to avoid making last-minute changes
- ❑ Don't leave issues unresolved; set timelines
- ❑ Allow them to make decisions
- ❑ Demonstrate urgency. Remember, J's tend to have a hurried pace, and a relaxed pace can be interpreted as wasting time!

▶ **If you both have a preference for J,** watch that you don't get overly-focused on closure! Use Perceiving to ask, "Could our decision be even better if we waited a bit?"

When they have a preference for P (Perceiving):

- ❑ Don't be annoyed if they arrive or finish just in time
- ❑ Focus more on the process than on organizing it
- ❑ Try being open to last-minute changes
- ❑ Get comfortable leaving issues open; don't set arbitrary deadlines
- ❑ Don't push them to make decisions, but expect questions and exploration
- ❑ Relax your pace. Remember, P's tend to have a casual pace, and a hurried demeanor can be interpreted as you rushing them!

▶ **If you both have a preference for P,** watch that you don't leave things open too long! Use Judging to ask, "Is it time for initial closure?"

So you've accomplished quite a lot!

- You now have an idea of your own four personality preferences
- You now have an idea of what your *opposite* four personality preferences are
- You've learned some type cues to help you identify the possible personality preferences of others, and
- You've learned some techniques for better communicating with people who have your opposite preferences, and some tips for optimizing interactions with people who have your same preferences

Our work is almost done! And what better way to end this book than with a story…

In the process of writing this book, I was acutely aware of practicing what I preach! I realized that if I didn't make a conscious effort to incorporate all eight personality preferences in the book, I would naturally write from just my own four preferences of E, N, F, and J. This would have likely been a delight for the people who also have those same exact four preferences. "I love the way he writes! He really speaks my language!" they'd say. But for anyone else with different preferences… well, probably not so much.

So here's what I attempted to do to engage each of the eight personality preferences:

Extraversion: I wrote in a conversational style, so that those of you who have a preference for E would feel like you weren't really reading – but instead, that you were actually having a conversation with me! Did you talk back?

Introversion: Since this *is* a book, which involves reading and processing internally, I figured we were good in the Introversion department! But I also baked in some questions here and there to engage your inner world and to give you the opportunity for reflection and contemplation.

Sensing: These stories are real, and that is about as Sensing as it gets! I also worked hard to describe the stories in detail and in sequential order, and to make sure each one had useful and practical application.

Intuition: Although the stories are real, I worked hard to include metaphors and word play, and also to "paint a picture" of each story. And the whole model of personality preferences is based on Jung's theory – and N's usually enjoy a good theory!

Thinking: My T friends would say that my subtle sarcasm appeals to those who have a preference for T! I also focused on putting these stories in a logical order, and to describe not only "perfect" stories of type, but times when type led to misunderstandings as well. In other words, I included both the good *and* the bad.

Feeling: There's plenty of opportunity to apply these stories to your own growth and development, as well as to the growth of the people you care about. And since these stories are about people and their interactions, I think we're good with F!

Judging: Structuring this book was easy, since the theory of personality preferences arranges the four aspects of personality in a predetermined order – which allowed this book to have a natural beginning, middle, and an end. Check, check, check!

Perceiving: Those of you who have a preference for Perceiving likely skipped around the book in your own way, starting in the middle, going to the end, then coming back to the beginning – so I figured all I needed to do was to include good content to make your Perceiving journey enjoyable!

By speaking the language of personality type, I do hope I was able to get through to each one of you. I also hope you've enjoyed these stories, and that the knowledge of personality type will enrich your life, your relationships, and your work as much as it has mine. Best wishes to you on your type journey!

Appendix

If you're interested in taking the official Myers-Briggs Type Indicator (MBTI) personality assessment, go to www.mbticomplete.com to take the assessment online.

To find an MBTI Master Practitioner to administer and/or interpret the MBTI assessment with you, see the MBTI Referral Network at www.mbtireferralnetwork.org.

To inquire about scheduling an MBTI workshop or speaking engagement with Patrick Kerwin, send an email to info@pkerwin.com.

Acknowledgements

Because this book is a collection of real stories from people in my personal life as well as people I've encountered in my work, it's no exaggeration to say, "This book truly would not have been possible without my incredible family, friends, colleagues, and MBTI workshop participants." Because of you, I never stop learning about type. And if you recognize yourself in one of these stories, thank you for helping others learn about type as well.

I want to extend special thanks to: Patti, for all of her unwavering support and incredible insights, and for always being willing to "talk type" with me; my sister Kathryn, her husband Nick, my nephew Alex, and my niece Delaney, for showing the beauty that type differences can bring into a family; Serena, for hours of amazing type conversations; Skyla and Phil, for your friendship; Rose, for always believing in me and for making me laugh; Sidney, for all the rich conversations about type and life; Helen, for helping me take my first steps into the depth of personality type; Gail and Barbs, for your amazing friendship; Les, Shannon, and Cindy, for all the thought-provoking discussions about type; all my friends at CPP, CAPT, and Psychometrics Canada; my friends in the MBTI community; to Alan, whose spirit lives forever within me; and Mrs. D, for all of your kindness and love.

Finally, I'd like to thank my partner Scott for all of his love and support both in our relationship and in the writing of this book. Being with you has taught me even more about the beauty of type differences, and is proof that opposites do indeed attract.

Made in the USA
San Bernardino, CA
22 February 2018